Essential Histories

The American Civil War

The war in the West 1861–July 1863

Essential Histories

The American Civil War

The war in the West 1861 – July 1863

Stephen D Engle

First published in Great Britain in 2001 by Osprey Publishing,
Elms Court, Chapel Way, Botley, Oxford OX2 9LP

Email: info@ospreypublishing.com

Every attempt has been made by the Publisher to secure the
appropriate permissions for material reproduced in this book. If
there has been any oversight we will be happy to rectify the
situation and written submission should be made to the
Publishers.

ISBN 1 84176 240 7

Editor: Rebecca Cullen
Design: Ken Vail Graphic Design, Cambridge, UK
Cartography by The Map Studio
Index by Susan Williams
Picture research by Image Select International
Origination by Grasmere Digital Imaging, Leeds, UK
Printed and bound in China by L. Rex Printing Company Ltd

01 02 03 04 05   10 9 8 7 6 5 4 3 2 1

For a complete list of titles available from Osprey Publishing
please contact:

Osprey Direct UK, PO Box 140,
Wellingborough, Northants, NN8 4ZA, UK
Email: info@ospreydirect.co.uk

Osprey Direct USA,
c/o Motorbooks International, PO Box 1,
Osceola, WI 54020-0001, USA.
Email: info@ospreydirectusa.com

www.ospreypublishing.com

Contents

Introduction: The nation in crisis

America in the mid-nineteenth century was a nation of conflicting ideological and cultural identities attempting to forge out of its agrarian traditions and industrial impulses a republic that remained committed to the ideals of its founding fathers. Bound by a common belief in freedom and independence as realized through democratic principles and republican virtues, Americans came to believe that their nation was God's chosen nation. However, although the country had been unified for more than 60 years, political, economic, social, and cultural differences stretching back to the nation's origins brought about a crisis for the young republic in 1861.

The development of an industrial society

In the early nineteenth century, the United States was predominantly an agrarian society. Land was fundamental to freedom, self-sufficiency, and independence. Most Americans believed that owning land and tilling the soil nurtured freedom and independence, and that those without land, engaged primarily in manufacturing, posed the greatest threat to that freedom. So long as land was plentiful, Americans believed, they could maintain the virtues granted them as the rightful beneficiaries of republican liberties. They could therefore escape poverty, dependency on others, and overpopulation produced by a manufacturing society. Thus, the desire to own land was at the core of the initial republican vision, as conceived by revolutionary leaders such as Thomas Jefferson.

Few Americans of Jefferson's generation, however, could have imagined that the quest for land that sparked the settlement of the west would actually accelerate rather than deter urban and industrial development. The very nature of the migration west was as much a cause as it was a consequence of the ideological differences and sectionalism that prevailed in the decades before the Civil War. Significantly, the migration and settlement of the west transformed an agrarian society that defined itself as a virtuous farming republic into an industrial society that came to accept the free-labor ideology as paramount in achieving republican dreams of a truly free and democratic society.

Beginning in the 1820s, westward expansion flowed along America's natural arteries, such as the Ohio and Mississippi Rivers and their tributaries, which allowed western farmers to channel goods south to New Orleans. After the 1830s, however, steamboats, canals, and railroads redirected western trade to the flourishing urban markets of the northeast. By the 1850s, over 60 percent of western foodstuffs were being shipped to the east. The cumulative impact of more effective transportation resulted in widening market opportunities. Simultaneously, the small manufacturing initiatives shifted from artisan shops to small factories, and merchant capitalists in the northeastern cities assumed the lead in organizing production for the expanding markets. In the four decades before the Civil War, urbanization and manufacturing reinforced each other in their growth patterns and came to shape the character of the North.

Although Southern whites moved west for basically the same reasons that Northerners did, the consequences of their move were different because of the presence of slavery. The cotton industry was directly linked to the size and substance of slave plantations. Between 1790 and 1860, cotton production exploded from 3,000 bales to 4,500,000 bales. Like the farmers of the Old Northwest who responded optimistically to market opportunities, planters and ambitious slaveholders responded to market incentives. Still, the slaveholder had little incentive to invest in labor-saving machinery and instead invested in land and slaves.

The antebellum wests, North and South, played integral roles in the economic

Like the Mississippi and Ohio Rivers, the Tennessee and Cumberland Rivers had been arteries of economic exchange in the decades before the Civil War, but the outbreak of war changed them into routes of military invasion. (*Harper's Weekly*, public domain)

development of the nation because they were linked to eastern markets. By the 1840s, the west had become a principal market for eastern manufactured goods and provided the cheap foodstuffs that fed the increasing numbers of factory workers who were being pulled to northern cities by employment. Cotton accounted for over 50 percent of the value of all American exports after the mid-1830s. More than any other commodity, cotton paid for American imports and served as the basis for national credit. Still, as the northeastern economy continued to develop and diversify, the economy of the South remained predominantly agrarian.

These east–west connections brought about by economic changes galvanized and shaped antebellum American culture and spawned a transportation revolution that brought not only numerous Americans into the market place, but also new expectations. The revolution in transport encouraged economic diversification, ethnic diversity, and an emphasis on free labor. These gave rise to an American middle class characterized by a materialism and moralism that sought to democratize the market place. Middle-class ideals harmonized with the Protestant work ethic to shape an environment conducive to capitalist

expansion. This Protestant ethic prompted many Northerners to embrace reform movements that sought to regulate society by helping persons who lacked self-control. By the 1850s, they had targeted the containment of slavery as one of their primary interests.

The South was largely untouched by the social and ideological consequences of the market revolution that spawned a middle class and its reforming zeal in the North. Though there was a small aspiring middle class of merchants, professionals, and tradesmen in the South, the region was bound to an agricultural slave society that repudiated the concepts of self-restraint and the celebration of the wage earner.

The challenge to slavery

In a republic that lacked any uniform concept of citizenship, an interpretive consensus of the Constitution, and a large standing army and navy, and where liberty and slavery coexisted, perhaps the only clearly defined aspect was that states possessed the exclusive rights to regulate slavery within their jurisdiction. By 1820, however, even those rights were being challenged. The congressional sessions of 1819 and 1820 concerning Missouri's admission to the Union as a slave state attested to the unsettling aspects of territorial expansion. The debates over slavery brought Northern frustrations about the institution to a climax and for the first time disclosed a bipartisan Northern majority determined to contain the institution. The conclusion of the debates produced the Missouri Compromise, which admitted Missouri as a slave state and Maine as a free state. Still, Missouri's southern boundary, the infamous 36–30 line, was extended westward through the remainder of the Louisiana Purchase territory. Above the imaginary line slavery was prohibited and below it the institution was permitted.

The combination of the financial panic of 1819 and the Missouri Compromise forced

The antebellum South was a land of prosperous cotton plantations. Even after the war, cotton remained king of agriculture. (Edimedia)

the fracture of the Republican Party. What emerged in its place was a Democratic Party that spoke to those who considered themselves victims of the ever-changing market place, and a Whig Party that spoke to those who considered themselves the winners or benefactors of the changing market place. By and large, Democrats, largely rural, championed a negative use of the government in the economy, attacked banks, opposed tariffs, and wanted to be left alone in their manners and morals. Whigs promoted a favorable and progressive use of the government in promoting economic change, and endorsed banks, higher tariffs, and free labor.

Ironically, in the pre-Civil War decades, these conflicting beliefs formed a strong concept of Union by averting the problems that threatened to dissolve it. However, they also allowed a significant degree of sectional strife to emerge. In 1832–33, in response to the tariff of 1828, South Carolina Planters led by John C. Calhoun forced a theory of nullification on the presidency of Andrew Jackson, whereby an individual state could nullify a federal law: that is, declare the law void within its borders. A crisis was averted as both sides compromised and claimed victory, but the significance of nullification was that Southerners came to believe they were a permanent minority. On the heels of Nat Turner's bloody slave uprising in Southampton, Virginia, in the summer of 1831, Southerners convinced themselves that their worst fears were before them. In the context of the Missouri Crisis, the Southern populace came to believe that the horror of losing independence could not be escaped. Concern over economic decline, combined with alarm over slave uprisings and the rise of abolition in the North, encouraged several Southern states to tighten slave codes and pass laws to suppress abolitionist speeches in the South.

The expansionist impulses of Americans, or 'Manifest Destiny' as it came to be known,

continued in the 1840s with the admission of Florida and Texas as slave states. The crisis over Texas's admission erupted in a war with Mexico that lasted two years and ended with the acquisition of Mexican territory. By gaining a land mass that nearly doubled the size of the United States, Americans faced the continuing dilemma of making the Federal government responsible for protecting the baggage of slavery that accompanied expansion.

By mid-century, American republicanism was facing a national crisis. The acquisition of Mexican land forced Americans to consider whether the newly expanded Union would be one with or without slavery. Land was losing its value in terms of promising

freedom and self-sufficiency because the freedom to earn a wage was gaining national prominence. Because the Democrats were the primary spokesmen for the original definition of freedom and advocates of the farmers, they came to the defense of Southern traditions. Whigs, on the other hand, came to view property as something earned in competition and supported free labor. As a prewar Whig, Abraham Lincoln espoused the virtues of free labor, remarking that 'There is no such thing as a man being bound down in a free country through his life as a laborer.'

In general, beginning in the 1840s, Northerners viewed the South as an impediment to realizing the full democratic principles that the market had to offer. Most anti-slavery Northerners opposed slavery not because of its effect on blacks, but because of the institution's effect on whites. It degraded the value of free labor. Southerners, however, came to believe that their fundamental rights were being usurped because they were a political minority. The Wilmot Proviso, which in 1846 unsuccessfully attempted to prohibit slavery in the territories, confirmed Southern fears that individual rights were no longer a constitutional matter, but a political matter. The emergence of the Free-Soil Party in the election of 1848, which promoted the containment of slavery, also helped to confirm these fears.

By the 1850s, Americans were searching for common ground that no longer existed in their political culture. Such a center had deteriorated through the accelerated pace of economic and social change after 1815 and the emotionally charged reactions to that change as a series of threatening conspiracies. The Compromise of 1850 was representative of the nature of congressional responses, attempting to placate both Northerners and Southerners. Although it admitted California as a free state, which offset the balance in the Senate in favor of Northern states, it also imposed a tougher Fugitive Slave Act. In many respects the Compromise of 1850 was at best an armistice to an American political culture attempting to wrest itself from permanent divisions along sectional lines.

The publication in 1852 of *Uncle Tom's Cabin*, a best-selling anti-slavery novel by Harriet Beecher Stowe, further intensified the emotionally charged atmosphere surrounding slavery. It hardened Northern middle-class attitudes regarding slavery's incompatibility with the nation's democratic principles. So popular and offensive was the book that, at one point during the Civil War when Abraham Lincoln finally met Harriet Beecher Stowe, he referred to her as 'the little lady who made this big war.'

Sectional tensions erupted in 1854 when the Kansas–Nebraska Act repealed the Missouri Compromise and allowed the ambiguous concept of 'popular sovereignty' (let the people of the territories decide) to settle the question of whether or not slavery would exist. When it passed, Illinois Senator Stephen A. Douglas prophesied that the Kansas–Nebraska Act would 'raise a hell of a storm.' Although it opened the landscape for the construction of a transcontinental railroad, it signaled the collapse of the Whig Party, served as a catalyst for the new Republican Party, and was instrumental in the growth of the one-party Democratic South.

In 1857, the Supreme Court attempted to settle the issue that Congress had failed to solve. By ruling in the Dred Scott case that Congress had no right to single out slave property for prohibition in the territories (areas owned by the US government but not yet divided into states), the Court endorsed what Southerners had believed all along – slavery was protected by the Constitution. Many Northerners concluded that politically a slave power did exist and that it had won a triumphant victory over the forces of free soil and free labor.

The issue of the territories was so central to the future of the republic and had become so politicized that the religious culture divided into factions. Church members came to believe in an anti-slavery God in the North and a pro-slavery God in the South. As institutional centers fragmented, the election of 1856 signaled a departure from an American culture forced to compromise repeatedly on issues of vital significance to the nation's future. Although James Buchanan won, the Democrats became unavoidably divided. Republicans employed the rhetoric of complete prohibition of slavery in the territories, and many white Southerners interpreted this as simply a disguise for the true intentions of the party to eventually abolish the institution.

In the debate over the territories, both parties claimed to be defending republican standards of individual freedom, liberty, honor, and moral righteousness. Yet, such fundamental disagreements, whether moral or political, over how these standards should be applied to the problems confronting the nation gave rise to hardening perceptions both of themselves and of each other by Northerners and Southerners. They became consumed by seeing one another as enemies.

By the end of the 1850s, hardened perceptions, emotionally charged legislative disputes, and vicious recriminations cast a mold of uncompromising attitude. In 1858, running for the Illinois senate, Lincoln perhaps best summed up the young republic's crisis in his famous 'House Divided' speech. 'I believe this government cannot endure, permanently half *slaves* and half *free*,' he concluded. The Civil War that erupted in 1861 revealed that Southerners and Northerners were fighting to preserve the fundamental patterns and practices of their economic and social life. What

Americans had failed to solve during peacetime, they would now settle by war.

A modern war

In many respects, the Civil War was a watershed in the history of warfare, as it ultimately took shape as a total or modern war. The warring sides voiced the rhetoric of ideology and cause, they employed conscription, simplified strategies and tactics to create armies of unparalleled size and power, and they used these armies to strike at the enemy and destroy their possessions. At first, Northern commanders anticipated a limited, short, and bloodless war that would restore the Union without alienating the Southern populace. They attempted to quickly prevail by blockading Southern ports and by capturing principal cities, including the Confederate capital, Richmond. By the end of 1861, however, Northern political leaders had come to believe that Union armies were actually losing the war because they were trying to win the peace.

Perhaps more than any other aspect of the war, rifled weapons gave rise to a longer and more protracted war. These rifles gave the armies a defensive advantage, and Northern soldiers soon realized that they could neither easily destroy Southern armies nor capture fortified positions. By early 1862, commanders fully understood the lethal implications of such firepower, at a time when Northern political leaders came to embrace an expansive war to be waged against the South's institutions. Northern political leaders and commanders sought not only to reduce Confederate forces in campaigns of attrition, but also to deplete the South's ability to wage war by liberating slaves, destroying the region's farms and factories, and most significantly, breaking the spirit of the Southern people.

The Civil War ravaged the American landscape for four years and instead of conserving the old America it steadily and profoundly reshaped the political, economic, and social contours of the nation. By the

South Carolina Senator John C. Calhoun, who devised the theory of nullification, was also an ardent defender of slavery. 'I hold that in the present state of civilization,' he once argued, 'the relation now existing in the slave-holding states between the two [races] is, instead of an evil, a good – a *positive* good.' (Ann Ronan Picture Library)

time it ended, the original American republic was gone. The postwar republic would be carved out of a world that the war made.

This third volume devoted to the American Civil War in the Osprey Essential Histories series focuses on the war in the Western Theater from the outbreak of the conflict to the surrender of Vicksburg, Mississippi, in July 1863. The region in which this war was fought stretches from the Appalachian Mountains west across Kentucky, Tennessee, Alabama, Mississippi, Louisiana, and across the Mississippi to Missouri and Arkansas. During the first two and a half years, the struggle for the Confederate heartland in the west was two-dimensional. As the Union and Confederate armies fought one brand of war to gain territory and defeat one another, the Southern residents and Union soldiers fought a different kind of war to maintain supremacy in the occupied zones.

Harriet Beecher Stowe, author of *Uncle Tom's Cabin*, spent just one weekend in a slave state and yet from Maine wrote the most popular novel of slavery of the nineteenth century. Her portrayal of slavery's cruelty sold over 300,000 books in America, and so powerful was her depiction of the slave trade that it brought tears to Queen Victoria's eyes. (Ann Ronan Picture Library)

Chronology

1820   Missouri Compromise divides the US territory into free territory and slave territory

1828   South Carolina politician John Calhoun urges nullification in response to the 1828 tariff

1836   Congress adopts the Gag Resolution on slavery

1845   Texas and Florida are admitted to the Union

1846–48 War against Mexico

1846   Pennsylvanian Congressman David Wilmot issues a proviso prohibiting slavery from territory acquired from Mexico

1850   Compromise of 1850 settles territorial issues and enacts a tough Fugitive Slave Law

1852   Publication of Harriet Beecher Stowe's *Uncle Tom's Cabin*

1854   Passage of the Kansas–Nebraska Act repeals the Missouri Compromise

1857   US Supreme Court rules that Dred Scott is not a citizen and Congress is powerless to prohibit slavery in the territories

1859   John Brown raids the federal armory and arsenal at Harpers Ferry in anticipation of arming Virginia slaves

1860   **6 November** Abraham Lincoln is elected President
        20 December South Carolina secedes from the Union

1861   **9 January–1 February** The remaining six states of the Lower South secede
        4 February–11 March Convention of delegates from the seceded states in Montgomery, Alabama, writes a constitution and selects Jefferson Davis and Alexander H. Stephens as provisional President and Vice-President of a Confederates States of America
        4 March Lincoln is inaugurated as President
        12–14 April Confederate bombardment results in the surrender of Fort Sumter
        15 April Lincoln calls for 75,000 volunteers to suppress the rebellion
        17 April–8 June Virginia, Tennessee, Arkansas, and North Carolina secede as a result of Lincoln's call for volunteers
        11 May Camp Jackson affair, St Louis, Missouri
        20 May Confederate Congress votes to move national government from Montgomery, Alabama, to Richmond, Virginia; Kentucky declares neutrality
        25 July US Senate passes Crittenden Compromise that the Union is not fighting to interfere with slavery
        10 August Battle of Wilson's Creek or Oak Hills, Springfield, Missouri
        30 August John C. Fremont declares martial law and declares slaves in Missouri free
        3 September Confederate forces under Gideon Pillow enter Kentucky, ending neutrality in that state
        10 September Confederate Albert Sidney Johnston is appointed to command Tennessee, Missouri, Arkansas, and Kentucky
        1 November George B. McClellan replaces Winfield Scott as General-in-Chief of the Armies
        6 November Jefferson Davis is elected provisional President by the people of the Confederacy
        9 November Don Carlos Buell and Henry Halleck are appointed to departments in Kentucky and Missouri
        2 December The second session of the thirty-seventh US Congress opens

1862   **19 January** Battle of Mill Springs or Logan's Cross Roads, Kentucky
6 February Union gunboats force the surrender of Fort Henry, Tennessee
13–16 February Battle of Fort Donelson, Tennessee, results in the Union's capture of 15,000 Confederates
26 February Don Carlos Buell captures Nashville, Tennessee
7–8 March Battle of Pea Ridge or Elkhorn Tavern, Arkansas
11 March Lincoln's War Order no. 3 relieves McClellan as General-in-Chief and consolidates western commands under Halleck
6–7 April Battle of Shiloh or Pittsburg Landing
16 April Confederate Congress passes the first National Conscription Act in American history
26 April Union gunboats force New Orleans to surrender
30 May Confederates evacuate Corinth, Mississippi
6 June Confederate surrender at Memphis, Tennessee
19 June Lincoln signs a law prohibiting slavery in the territories
11 July Halleck is named General-in-Chief of the US Army
13 July General Nathan Bedford Forrest captures Murfreesboro, Tennessee
17 July Second Confiscation Act approved by US Congress
30 August Battle of Richmond, Kentucky, launches Braxton Bragg's invasion into Kentucky
17 September Battle of Munfordville, Kentucky
19 September Battle of Iuka, Mississippi
22 September Lincoln announces preliminary Emancipation Proclamation
4 October Battle of Corinth, Mississippi
8 October Battle of Perryville or Chaplin Hills, Kentucky
20 October Lincoln orders John McClernand to raise troops for an expedition against Vicksburg, Mississippi
24 October William Rosecrans replaces Buell as commander of Union forces in Kentucky and Tennessee
24 November Joseph E. Johnston is assigned to Confederate command in the west
7 December Battle of Prairie Grove, Arkansas
20 December Confederates under Earl Van Dorn raid Holly Springs, Mississippi
31 December–3 January Battle of Murfreesboro or Stone's River, Tennessee

1863   **1 January** Lincoln issues Emancipation Proclamation
11 January Federal gunboats capture Fort Hindman, Arkansas
30 January Ulysses S. Grant assumes command of the expedition against Vicksburg, Mississippi
25 February US Congress passes the National Banking Act
3 March US Congress passes the National Enrollment Act, which institutes a national draft
7 March Nathaniel Banks' Federal force moves to Baton Rouge to cooperate with Grant's Vicksburg expedition
17 April Confederate Benjamin Grierson launches a raid into Mississippi to draw attention from Grant's expedition
24 April Confederate Congress enacts the Tax-in-Kind Law, which requires agricultural producers to give a portion of various crops to the national government
1 May Battle of Port Gibson, Mississippi
14 May Engagement at Jackson, Mississippi
16 May Battle of Champion's Hill, Mississippi
18 May–4 July Siege of Vicksburg, Mississippi
9 July The fall of Port Hudson

The North and South compared

Although some contemporaries of the conflict, as well as some later scholars, claimed that the war was inevitable, neither side had prepared for the conflict. Neither Northerners nor Southerners could foresee the consuming force of mobilization that affected both men and materials. Secessionists were, however, correct in believing that the South had been reduced to minority status. The fact that 23 states, including four border slave states, supported the Union and only 11 states joined the Confederacy was confirmation alone of the accuracy of that perception.

With a total population in the United States of roughly 31.5 million people, once the political lines were drawn the Union comprised about 22.5 million people, of whom 3.5 million constituted a manpower pool for the armed forces. The Confederacy contained slightly over 9.1 million persons, of whom 3.5 million were slaves, leaving a manpower pool of roughly 1 million available for the armed forces. This constituted about 55 percent of the white population of military age serving in the Union armies.

The 4 to 1 edge in manpower was matched by some significant material contrasts between the North and South. Industrially, the North out-produced the South 10 to 1 in gross value of manufacturing. The Tredegar Iron Works in Richmond, Virginia, was the Confederacy's only major industrial factory. Tredegar's existence strengthened the Confederacy's will to defend its capital. The North's factories manufactured 97 percent of the nation's firearms and 96 percent of its railroad equipment. In the production of locomotives and firearms, the Union advantage was in excess of 25 to 1. Whether measured by the size of manufacturing or manpower, the ability to replace or replenish

industrial equipment destroyed in the course of the war clearly favored the North. Moreover, a majority of the country's textiles, shoes, iron products, and coal, corn and wheat came from Northern factories. In addition, the number of financial institutions and the value of bank deposits also favored the Union roughly 4 to 1.

Even in farm production the Northern states overwhelmed the Confederacy, as a majority of the citizens tilled the soil for a living. Northerners tilled 75 percent of the country's farm acreage, tended 60 percent of the nation's livestock, and harvested nearly 70 percent of its corn and 80 percent of its wheat. As the progress of the war upset Southern output, Northern farms managed to increase productivity, despite losing workers to the army. The Confederacy produced enough to meet minimal needs, but disruption along the rivers and rails caused shortages in many places. Meanwhile, the North produced a surplus of wheat for export at a time when drought and crop failures in Europe created a critical demand. Wheat became king during the war and supplanted cotton as the nation's major export, becoming the chief means of acquiring foreign money and bills of exchange to pay for imports from abroad.

The North's advantage in transport weighed heavily as the war went on. The Union had more wagons, horses, mules, and ships than the Confederacy, and an impressive edge in railroads of 2 to 1. The discrepancy was even greater, for Southern railroads were mainly short lines built to different gauges, and had few replacements for rolling stock that frequently broke down. The Confederacy had only one east–west connection, between Memphis and Chattanooga. The latter was an important rail hub with connections through Knoxville, into Virginia and down through Atlanta to Charleston and Savannah. Western farmers found numerous outlets to the eastern seaboard during the war, which lessened their dependence on the Mississippi River.

Perhaps the Union's greatest advantage was its potential to harness effectively the war machine that its economic superiority allowed it, since it was able to use and replenish war materials effectively if the war was long. Though small in number and pathetically underequipped, the Union began with at least some semblance of a professional army and navy. At the outbreak of the war, the United States army had 14,000 soldiers and 42 ships. The Confederate government, on the other hand, was forced to create in the midst of the war not only an army and navy, but also the industrial base to produce such entities.

Still, several factors served to reduce the material superiority of the Union and favor the Confederacy. The sheer size of the 750,000 square miles (nearly 2 million km²) of the Confederacy alone proved ominously perplexing for the Union. History provided lessons that countries far smaller than the Confederacy could successfully win or maintain their independence against invaders with larger armies and more material resources. The landscape was not only vast but also diverse, which made penetrating the interior of the region more complicated the further south Union armies traveled. If the Union were to attempt invasion over land or by sea, which stretched for 3,500 miles (5,600km), this could be difficult. Control of rivers and rails as well as strategic junctions meant that large armies would have not only to defeat the enemy, but also to occupy significant portions of the land to secure what they had conquered. The early

campaigns in the west would necessitate changes in how Union armies conducted themselves as occupiers of Southern soil. Union soldiers had to protect supply lines, transportation and communication centers, and pacify the citizenry while administering loyalty oaths and protecting Southern Unionists from Confederate retribution.

The second advantage for the South was the defensive nature of the war itself. The Confederacy's primary strategic goal was to defend the territory that it held at the outbreak of war and to prolong the conflict until the Union grew weary of war and acknowledged Confederate independence. Unlike the Union, which sought the political objective of reunion, Southerners did not have to subjugate Northerners. Victory or even stalemate on the battlefields would more than likely have resulted in the

This hand-colored lithograph of the Union high command reveals the stark contrast between George B. McClellan and Winfield Scott, who sit on opposite sides of a council of war. Portrayed here from left to right are McClellan, Silas H. Stringham, Irvin McDowell, Franz Sigel, John E. Wool, John A. Dix, Nathaniel Banks, Samuel P. Heintzelman, Scott, Robert Anderson, John C. Fremont, and Benjamin Butler. (Anne S. K. Brown Military Collection, Brown University Library)

Confederacy's independence. The Northern aims of conquest required far more troops than the defensive war pursued by the Confederacy. Fighting against invasion tended to elevate morale and also allowed the armies the advantage of utilizing the topography that was familiar to them.

The third major factor that enabled the Confederacy to reduce the material odds against its armies was the presence of slavery. Southern whites concluded that the slaves themselves provided a decided military advantage. They freed up considerable manpower to fill the volunteer ranks, provided the unskilled labor left behind, produced the foodstuffs, worked as laborers, teamsters, boatmen, and cooks, and were responsible for repairing railroads and bridges, and reconstructing cities destroyed by Union armies. Still, even with the assistance of slaves,

roughly 75 percent of Southern white males of military age served in the Confederate armies.

Perhaps more influential in determining the war's outcome than material imbalances and geographical advantages were the soldiers and commanders themselves. Although many commanders North and South shared an identical military heritage, more often than not generals alone could determine the difference between success and failure. To sustain a total commitment to the cause required effective leadership, not only from Washington or Richmond but also from the ranks. Although Lincoln and Davis shared some military credentials – Davis was a graduate of West Point and participated in the Mexican War, and Lincoln had served in the Black Hawk War of the 1830s – neither man was prepared for the daunting task required of a commander-in-chief during wartime.

While Davis was hardworking and committed to the cause, his temperament was not well suited to his new post. He possessed a weakness for friends and gave them special consideration, sometimes against his better judgement. He took his role as commander-in-chief literally and frequently interfered with commanders. To further complicate his task, Davis faced an institutional crisis. Because the Confederacy had been founded on the ideology of states' rights, the demands of war would require that he strengthen the authority of the central government beyond anything that the South would accept. Lincoln, on the other hand, was a shrewd judge of character and was not as proprietary over his generals or armies. Leading a nation instead of states greatly advantaged him in controlling Northern armies. Although frequently the target of scathing attacks, Lincoln never wavered in his ability to see the larger political objectives of the war and seldom allowed personal feelings to blind him. 'This is essentially a People's contest,' he asserted at the beginning of the war, and he never let the populace or the commanders forget this fact.

Although economic factors dictated that Europe, particularly Great Britain, stay out of

This photograph captures Mississippi recruits being mustered in at the Natchez courthouse in early 1861. Mississippi's military population at the outbreak of the Civil War was estimated to be 70,000. (Review of Reviews Company)

the contest, so did considerations of power politics, despite the fact that the British imported more than 80 percent of its cotton from the American South. British officials recognized the legality of the Confederacy as well as the legality of the Union blockade, but the North probably benefited more from Britain's neutrality than the Confederacy.

In the end, the very nature of the Civil War would reveal much about the societies waging it. It was indeed a 'people's contest', and essentially the military regiments were small communities at war. Ultimate victory would be won by the nation that effectively marshaled its resources, maintained popular support for the war, developed a strategic plan that blended political and military objectives, and possessed the economic endurance to stay the course. The fact that they would come to believe much about themselves through the experience of war was as much a consequence as it was a cause of war.

A nation at war

The combination of financial depression resulting from the panic of 1857, the Supreme Court's Dred Scott ruling, and the crisis in Kansas loomed ominously over the Buchanan administration. In October 1859, however, his presidency suffered another blow. John Brown, who had made the cause of anti-slavery his never-ending crusade, attempted to single-handedly purge slavery from Virginia. On 16 October, Brown and his small band of followers raided and seized the small government arsenal at Harpers Ferry, Virginia, in an attempt to arm the slaves and launch an insurrection against slaveholders. Two days later Robert E. Lee arrived, accompanied by a detachment of Marines. They surrounded the arsenal and either killed or wounded the vigilantes associated with Brown. Brown himself was captured, tried for treason, and hanged on 2 December.

Despite his failed attempt, Brown would be forever martyred for the anti-slavery cause. Republicans scurried to disassociate themselves from Brown's actions. Still, it became evident that Brown's scheme had been supported by a small group of Boston abolitionists, who came to be known as the

'Without shedding of blood there is no remission [of sin]' was John Brown's favorite biblical passage. It inspired him to seize the Federal Armory and Arsenal at Harpers Ferry, Virginia, in mid-October 1859 and to launch a massive slave insurrection. The attempt failed and Brown met his fate on the gallows on 2 December in Charles Town, Virginia. (Ann Ronan Picture Library)

LOUDON HEIGHTS.

HARPER'S FERRY.

MARYLAND HEIGHTS.

Secret Six. Though not one of the six, abolitionist Wendell Phillips supported Brown, proclaiming, '[Virginia] is a pirate ship, and John Brown sails the sea a Lord High Admiral of the Almighty with his commission to sink every pirate he meets on God's ocean of the nineteenth century.' Brown's attempt and the elevation of him for his sacrifice to the abolitionist cause incensed Southern whites.

In this rigid atmosphere of gridlock politics and rule-or-ruin attitudes came the election of 1860. Democrats convened in Charleston, South Carolina. Failing to win a majority of non-slaveholding Democrats to their side in the legislature, the Southern extremists chose instead to emphasize secession if a Republican were elected the next president. Led by William L. Yancy of Alabama, they boldly demanded that the party endorse the protection of slavery in the territories in its national platform. If their demand was rejected, they were prepared to leave the convention. The North's most popular Democratic candidate was Stephen A. Douglas, who, seeking to contend for Northern votes against the Republicans, rejected the slave platform. The Lower South delegates left the convention. In June, when the party reconvened in Baltimore, the regular Democrats finally nominated Douglas. Southern Democrats meanwhile nominated Kentucky slaveholder John C. Breckinridge and endorsed a platform that included a federal slave code.

As the fractured Democratic Party battled over its nomination for president, die-hard Whigs and Know Nothings (an anti-immigrant party) formed the Constitutional Union Party and nominated Tennessean John C. Bell for president. Bell was a life-long Whig and his party adopted a platform that pledged its support for the Union and a love of the Constitution. The party appealed primarily to Upper South states, whose citizens simply wanted to avoid any conflict that would force them to choose between loyalty and locality.

The Republicans convened in May in Chicago and nominated Abraham Lincoln as

The pattern of voting between Lincoln and Breckinridge reveals very closely the division between Union and Confederate governments. Note that the slave states of Tennessee, Kentucky, and Virginia voted for Bell.

their presidential candidate. An ex-Whig who had been out of politics for more than a decade, and who had few enemies, Lincoln appeared the perfect choice. The Republicans endorsed a platform that focused on economic issues and promised a better future. By advocating its opposition to the spread of slavery in the territories, and supporting it in the states, the party leaders could avoid being dubbed the party of abolition. However, if a Republican won the White House, many Southerners concluded, it was simply a matter of time before the institution of slavery lost its constitutional support.

The election was a sectionalized contest between the North, which held a majority of the electoral votes and pitted Lincoln and Douglas against each other, and the South, which pitted Breckinridge against John Bell. Although Lincoln and Douglas accounted for nearly 90 percent of the vote in the North, in the South Douglas won only Missouri, and Lincoln was not even on the ballot in 10 slave states. Breckinridge and Bell received over 85 percent of the Southern popular vote and barely over 10 percent in the North. Significantly, however, the Constitutional Union candidate, Bell, carried only three Upper South states – Virginia, Kentucky, and Tennessee. In the end, Lincoln received only 40 percent of the popular vote, but gained the North's 180 electoral votes. Still, the Republicans had not won control of either house of Congress. Shortly after the election, Republican editor and writer William Cullen Bryant boasted that 'the cause of justice and liberty has triumphed,' and although the people of South Carolina were making such a fuss about the result, Bryant confided, 'I have not the least apprehension that anything serious will result from it.'

Southern fears escalated beyond reasonable proportions, however, as many Southerners interpreted the results as a

The election of 1860

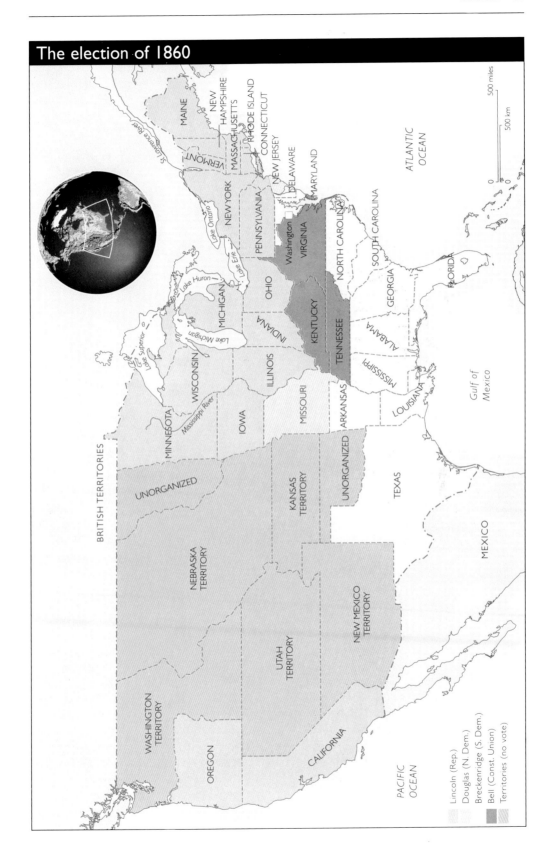

Jefferson Davis was sworn in as the Confederacy's first provisional president on 18 February 1861, on the steps of the capitol building of Montgomery, Alabama. 'Upon my ... head were showered smiles, plaudits and flowers,' Davis recalled, 'but beyond them I saw troubles.' (Ann Ronan Picture Library)

victory for free labor and an end to slavery. Secession appeared the only alternative to protest the election. South Carolina, which had been embroiled in the nullification controversy some 30 years before, was the first to act, unanimously seceding from the Union on 20 December 1860. As Congress prepared to respond, six other Lower South states would also secede during the course of the next six weeks: Mississippi, Florida,

Alabama, Georgia, Louisiana, and Texas. Together the states organized the Confederate States of America at Montgomery, Alabama, in February 1861. They elected Mississippian Jefferson Davis and Georgian Alexander Stephens as president and vice-president respectively. Never before in American history had more work of such monumental significance been done in such little time. One Southern newspaper declared: 'The North and South are heterogeneous and we are better apart ... we are doomed if we proclaim not our political independence.'

Before Lincoln was even sworn in as president, these states adopted a constitution and charted a course for complete independence. By casting themselves as the revolutionaries, secessionists legitimized their actions and placed themselves in the role of the defenders of individual liberties. Secessionists effectively portrayed Republicans as symbols of threatening economic and social change, and greedy capitalists intent on forcing Southern whites into wage slavery. With Lincoln about to take office, Southerners adopted a constitution that not only protected slavery, but also allowed states more power than the Confederate government.

President James Buchanan meanwhile remained in office, content to believe that secession was illegitimate. He hoped that Congress would produce a compromise, but when none was forthcoming, he stood by as the seceded states seized federal forts that skirted the Southern coast from South Carolina to Texas. Although eight slave states still remained in the Union, they vowed to remain only as long as Lincoln guaranteed the protection of the institution where it existed and pledged not to invade the seceded states.

As Lincoln prepared to take office after four long and eventful months, he was willing to allow the stalemate to continue, hoping for a solution, perhaps a voluntary reunion, perhaps simply more time. Lincoln's inaugural speech placed responsibility for the crisis squarely on the shoulders of the Confederates. He made it clear that he intended to uphold his federal responsibilities by protecting federal property, 'but beyond what may be necessary for these objects,' he assured the Confederates, 'there will be no invasion.'

Although there were interpretive differences over just what the President would do, a crisis in Charleston, South Carolina, presented him with little time. One of the few remaining federal garrisons in the South, Fort Sumter, was in need of supplies or it would have to surrender in six weeks. Hoping to give as much time to the peace process as possible, Lincoln delayed making a decision about the fort. With time running

out, however, he had to act not only to save the garrison but also to legitimize his leadership in the crisis. On 4 April, Lincoln, convinced that Major Robert Anderson's garrison could no longer hold out, decided to resupply Fort Sumter. While both Lincoln and Davis hoped to avoid being the aggressor in the crisis, Lincoln's determination now shifted the burden of decision to Jefferson Davis.

On 9 April, the Confederate President assembled his cabinet, which decided against allowing the fort to be supplied. With federal supplies on the way, Davis instructed Pierre G. T. Beauregard, commander of the Confederate forces in Charleston, to demand the surrender of the fort. When Anderson refused the ultimatum, Beauregard's Confederate batteries began shelling the fort early in the morning of 12 April. The bombardment lasted some 33 hours before Anderson capitulated. As the victors lowered the American flag, the Palmetto flag was raised in its place, signaling the shift in possession of the fort.

The showdown at Sumter prompted Lincoln to call for the loyal states to supply 75,000 militiamen to suppress the rebellion. As volunteers flocked to the recruiting stations throughout the North, residents in the Upper South, known as the border states, decided in favor of secession. Lincoln's call for volunteers, as Southerners interpreted it, had clearly violated his inaugural pledge, and the states of Virginia, Arkansas, North Carolina, and Tennessee protested this action by voting to join the Confederacy. The Confederate capital was moved to Richmond. The Union's loss of these states to the Confederacy complicated political attitudes, and residents were torn between conflicting loyalties. There appeared to be significant pockets of loyal support in the border states, particularly those in the west. The fact that Kentucky, the native state of both Lincoln and Davis, attempted to remain neutral revealed much about the complex interplay between loyalty and location. Most at stake were the vital resources and manpower of the states,

'Plainly, the central idea of secession is the essence of anarchy,' Lincoln argued in his inaugural address. 'A majority, held in restraint by constitutional checks, and limitations … is the only true sovereign of a free people.' (Ann Ronan Picture Library)

which could clearly tip the scales between victory and defeat.

With 11 slave states out of the Union, the American republic had succumbed to the fundamental conflict it had wrestled with since acquiring independence from Great Britain. Clearly the ideological and political struggle to maintain the diverse cords of slave labor and free labor as well as states'

rights and federal supremacy had been weakened as they played out on a number of stages in the decades before the war. Now they had broken, and the Union would never be the same. 'Civil War is freely accepted everywhere,' declared a Bostonian a week after the firing on Fort Sumter. Indeed it was and as Orrin Mortimer Stebbins, a Pennsylvania schoolteacher concluded, 'We live in an age of rebellion … I can only say that I live for the Stars and Stripes, *and for them I am ready to die!!!'* The four long years that followed would be evidence that the United States was in a defining period.

Struggle for the heartland

The Western Theater, delineated by the Appalachian Mountains in the east and the Mississippi River in the west, also included the states of Missouri and Arkansas. The states that were most perplexed about how to proceed at the outbreak of war included Kentucky, Tennessee, and Missouri. The fact that the Ohio and Mississippi Rivers, as well as two significant tributaries, the Cumberland and the Tennessee, flowed through this region made it all the more significant as a war zone. 'Whatever Nation gets … control of the Ohio, Mississippi, and Missouri Rivers,' concluded Union General William T. Sherman, 'will control the continent.'

This region was settled largely by Southerners, but it was tied geographically and economically to the Ohio and Mississippi river valleys. This meant that economic exchanges with Northern markets were commonplace and thus a shared regional identity took shape in the pre-Civil War decades. Nowhere were loyalties more divided and the term a 'brother's war' more applicable than in the west. John L. Crittenden, the Kentucky politician who proposed the Crittenden Compromise months before, would have two sons who fought on opposite sides.

Volunteers came from all over the United States and filled the ranks of both armies as

Note the maze of rivers and railroads that afforded Union and Confederate armies strategic avenues to campaign in the west.

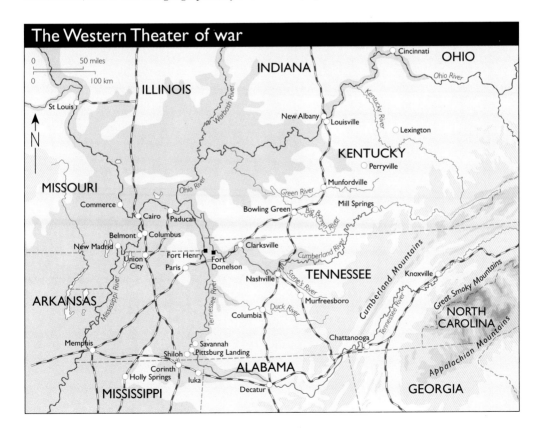

The Western Theater of war

soon as the war broke out. Some
700,000 men mustered into the Northern
armies during the initial months of the war.
Most enlisted for three years' service. Out of
approximately 1 million white males of
military age, the Confederate Congress called
on 500,000 men to enlist, which inspired
hundreds of thousands to muster into
service. Roughly 50 percent signed up for
three years and the other half enlisted
for 12 months.

Companies of 100 soldiers constituted the
primary unit of organization on both sides.
Theoretically, 10 companies made up a
regiment, four or more regiments comprised a
brigade, two or more brigades comprised a
division, and two or more divisions comprised
a corps. Companies and regiments were
frequently raised from single communities
and their officers were typically leaders in
those communities. Officers with experience
or education were frequently commanders of
brigades, divisions, corps, and armies.

As armies began to take shape, so did
military strategy. Reunion of Northerners
and Southerners was the principal goal of
Northern political and military leaders.
Preservation of the Union was paramount to
Union war aims, and politicians and
commanders planned to fight a limited war
for limited goals. By pledging to protect
noncombatants and by respecting their
constitutional guarantees (a strategy
intended to attract Southerners back to the
Union), the Union army could concentrate
on fighting the Confederate army. But
between 1861 and 1863, the means for
obtaining reunion changed dramatically. The
experience of fighting in the west brought
about fundamental political and military
changes that shifted and broadened Union
war aims. Over time, winning the war
became more important than winning
the peace.

General-in-Chief Winfield Scott initially
devised a strategic plan for the Union. The
'Anaconda Plan,' as it was known, called for
Union forces to move down the Mississippi
River and split the Confederacy, while
blockading Southern ports in an attempt to

strangle the economy. Scott's plan would require 300,000 well-trained men and would take two years to complete. Political and popular pressure to get the war moving, however, forced Scott to reconsider his overwhelming invasion plan. Still, using the waterways to strike at the Confederacy would ultimately prove to be a great advantage for the Union.

Because slavery and states' rights were central to Southern life, the Confederate war effort struggled with building a nation founded on these beliefs while attempting to fight a war that did not necessarily serve these interests. To wage a war that did not deliberately protect slavery and preserve states' rights would diminish popular support for the conflict. Confederate political

Camp Jackson, Missouri, was a suburb of St Louis and on 10 May 1861 it was the scene of a violent outbreak of war. After Nathaniel Lyon's troops had forced the surrender of Camp Jackson and its inhabitants, violence erupted that resulted in the death of 28 citizens. They were mainly bystanders, including women and children. (Review of Reviews Company)

and military leaders therefore sought to wage a defensive war. Protection of the South and its institutions from invading armies became the overall strategy for the war in the west.

The Union occupies Missouri

When Kentucky declared neutrality at the outbreak of the conflict, both Lincoln and Davis ordered military commanders to respect the state's dubious position. This meant that Northern penetration in the west would have to skirt Kentucky, and thus Northern armies would be forced to traverse the Appalachian Mountains to the east and the Mississippi River to the west, neither of which seemed feasible in the spring of 1861. Southerners feared that a neutral Kentucky might soon fall prey to the Union. Kentucky was indeed important. 'I think to lose Kentucky,' remarked Lincoln with obvious concern, 'is nearly to lose the whole game.' 'Kentucky gone, we can not hold Missouri, nor, as I think, Maryland. These all against us, and the job on our hands is too large for us.'

Whatever Kentucky's importance, while it remained neutral, little could be done in the Bluegrass state. Missouri then became all the more important for the Confederacy, as its border was just across the river from Kentucky. Missourians rejected secession in March and remained in the Union, but considering the heavy pro-South contingent in the southern part of the state and along the river, war came early to the western state. After rejecting Lincoln's call for volunteers in April, the secessionist Governor Claiborne Jackson, with the support of the pro-secessionist legislature, attempted to seize the federal arsenal and federal subtreasury in St Louis. On 10 May the rival factions came to blows at Camp Jackson, near St Louis, where Jackson's militia encamped. Federal Captain Nathaniel Lyon, a fiery, anti-slavery veteran of the earlier skirmishes in Kansas, captured the Confederate force and marched them through the streets of St Louis back to the arsenal. An angry pro-South mob

gathered and triggered a riot that left
28 civilians and two soldiers dead and
dozens more wounded.

Days later, Lyon and Jackson met to
discuss the future of Missouri in the hope of
avoiding more bloodshed. The meeting
ended when Lyon refused to concede to the
Governor's demands. 'Rather then
concede to the State of Missouri for one
instant the right to dictate to my
Government in any matter,' he defiantly

This lithograph shows Franz Sigel, the leader of
German-Americans in the war, who served under
Nathaniel Lyon during the Missouri campaign, being
inspired by Lyon, who was killed during the Battle of
Wilson's Creek. (Anne S. K. Brown Military Collection,
Brown University Library)

remarked, 'I would see you ... and every
man, woman, and child in the State, dead
and buried. *This means war.*'

Ironically, the move to suppress
Confederate sympathy had in fact fueled

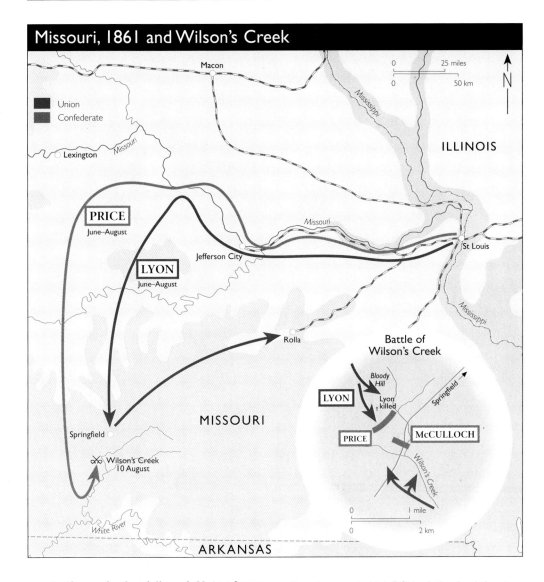

Missouri, 1861 and Wilson's Creek

war. In the weeks that followed, Union forces managed to push Jackson's militia toward the southwestern part of Missouri, capturing in the process the state capital at Jefferson City on 15 June. Lyon and Colonel Franz Sigel, a prominent German-American leader, pursued with about 5,500 men and occupied the town of Springfield. But Lyon's soldiers were at the end of a weak supply line with no promise of reinforcements. Soon the 8,000 secessionist militia led by Major-General Sterling Price were joined by 5,000 Confederate troops under Major-General Benjamin McCulloch. Lyon nevertheless refused to retreat and, learning

Once the secessionists left St Louis, they headed west along the Missouri River until the Union forces caught up with them and forced them into the southern part of the state near Springfield. On 10 August 1861, Union forces under Nathaniel Lyon fought the Confederates under Sterling Price and Benjamin McCulloch.

that the Rebels would soon launch an offensive, decided to attack first.

On 10 August the Union forces struck the Southerners at Wilson's Creek or Oak Hills, 10 miles (16km) south of Springfield. Lyon's attack was risky, but came close to success. The Rebel troops were poorly trained and equipped, and Lyon managed to achieve surprise with a daring two-pronged attack.

A confused savage battle ensued along the banks of Wilson's Creek. Lyon's men managed to hold their ground, in the face of nearly three-to-one odds, until Lyon was fatally wounded. The combination of Lyon's death and depleted ammunition forced the Federals to retreat. Eventually they fell back over 100 miles (160km) to Rolla, a railroad town that linked them to St Louis.

Union and Confederate forces both suffered roughly 1,300 casualties in this battle. In the weeks that followed, Confederates marched into the Missouri River valley, and they captured Lexington, Missouri, in mid-September. Thus, for a few months, Price's militia controlled half the state. The Confederate commander, however, soon discovered that he lacked the manpower to hold such a vast region, and in October he withdrew again to the southwest corner of Missouri. Although they had lost the key battle, the Federals ironically managed to hold on to Missouri, although their grip was tenuous and remained so until the next year. Throughout the war, Missouri was the battleground for continual and vicious guerrilla warfare.

Union advances in Kentucky

Meanwhile, in Kentucky, while both presidents attempted to steer armies around the state, secessionist Governor Beriah Magoffin also repudiated Lincoln's request for troops. Still, he allowed the Unionist legislature to exercise a degree of power throughout the summer. Nonetheless, recruiting for both sides went on in the state until Confederate fears over possible Union occupation of the region along the Mississippi River forced the Confederates to seize Columbus, Kentucky. Major-General Leonidas Polk was ordered to seize the strategic town, positioned on a high bluff overlooking the Mississippi River. Although he was prompted to strike because of the town's military importance, the political consequences were monumental. Declaring that the Confederacy had invaded the

George B. McClellan, commander of the Army of the Potomac and general-in-chief of the Union army from 5 November 1861 to 11 March 1862, was an advocate of fighting a limited war. He impressed this attitude on the commanders whom he appointed to commands in the west, including Don Carlos Buell and Henry Wager Halleck. (Ann Ronan Picture Library)

Bluegrass state, Kentucky's Union authorities pledged their support for the Union and forced Magoffin to resign. Federal forces under Major-General Ulysses S. Grant immediately occupied Paducah, Kentucky, near the mouth of the Tennessee River and connected to Columbus by railroad. Although the Union held only a thin strip of Kentucky's border, its strategic significance far outweighed its small size.

As in Missouri, Union and Confederate authorities moved quickly to shore up strategic points in the state. Federal forces immediately took Louisville, the largest city, and Frankfurt, the Kentucky capital. Major-General Robert Anderson commanded Louisville until he was replaced in September by Major-General William T. Sherman. As Union politicians contemplated how best to occupy the region they now held militarily, significant changes were occurring in military personnel.

In early November, Major-General George B. McClellan replaced General Winfield Scott

Henry Halleck was known in the regular army before the Civil War as 'Old Brains' for his impressive intellect. McClellan appointed him commander of the Department of Missouri in November 1861 and his leadership in the western campaigns so impressed Lincoln that he became the President's chief of staff in July 1862. (Massachusetts Commandery Military Order of the Loyal Legion and the US Army Military History Institute)

A close prewar friend of McClellan, who shared his superior's limited-war beliefs, Don Carlos Buell became commander of the Department of Ohio and played an instrumental role in bringing about success in the west. (Ann Ronan Picture Library)

as general-in-chief of the Union armies. McClellan was a youthful, self-absorbed, but vigorous and intelligent commander who shared the President's political and strategic vision of a limited war for limited goals. He moved quickly to stabilize the political and military situation in the west. He appointed like-minded commanders for the war's most important commands.

McClellan replaced John C. Fremont, who had issued an unauthorized emancipation proclamation in Missouri, with Major-General Henry Halleck. At 46, Halleck, a West Point graduate, had already demonstrated brilliance as a writer of military theory. When the war broke out, he was perhaps the most sought-after Union commander. He would be sent to St Louis to bring some semblance of order to the chaos. As a result of the reorganization of military departments in the west, Halleck would be responsible for the area that stretched westward from the Cumberland River through Missouri.

Major-General Don Carlos Buell commanded the newly organized Department of the Ohio, which included the region stretching from the Appalachian Mountains to the Cumberland River, but included all of Kentucky. Since his graduation from West Point in 1841, Buell was one of the few regular army officers in the western command and was a staunch advocate of limited war. He had acquired eight slaves through his prewar marriage and was a conservative Democrat, like McClellan and Halleck. McClellan thought that sending him to Kentucky might placate Kentuckians. Although its command in the west was divided, the Union had twice the number of troops as the Confederates with which to conduct affairs in the respective departments, which stretched some 500 miles (800km).

The Confederates meanwhile sought to unify the command of the western region

In 1861, Albert Sidney Johnston was regarded as one of the nation's finest military commanders, but his Civil War career was one of the great disappointments of the Confederacy. He was wounded at the Battle of Shiloh and bled to death while his staff physician was attending to wounded Southern and Northern soldiers. (Ann Ronan Picture Library)

under the leadership of Major-General Albert Sidney Johnston. A charismatic Texan, with outstanding credentials, having graduated from West Point eighth in his class and having served in the Black Hawk War, the Mexican War, and the Mormon War of 1858, Johnston was an excellent choice. Moreover, he was a good friend of President Davis. On his shoulders would fall the responsibility of defending the 500-mile (800km) line that stretched from the Appalachians to the Ozarks in the west across the Mississippi river. He constructed a defensive cordon that ran from Columbus on the Mississippi to Cumberland Gap in the Appalachians.

Besides the daunting task of defending such a vast line, Johnston was also strapped with the liability of having a core of subordinates whose authority exceeded their abilities. Polk, the commander of the western stronghold at Columbus, was also a West Point graduate, but left the military to become an Episcopal Bishop before the war.

On the extreme of the Confederate defensive line was Brigadier-General Felix Zollicoffer, a prewar journalist who advanced his Southern forces into eastern Kentucky. To block a Union invasion from Louisville, the Confederates occupied Bowling Green in the center of the state and command of the forces there went to Simon Bolivar Buckner. To assist in holding the front, Johnston had two political generals, Gideon Pillow and John B. Floyd, who proved wholly incompetent as military commanders.

Trying to defend a huge expanse of territory with inept leadership, Johnston's task was further handicapped by a lack of resources – a problem that would plague the Confederacy throughout the war. East of the Mississippi River, Johnston could concentrate at any one place only about 45,000 men, and west of the river, perhaps 15,000 soldiers. Still, once they occupied Kentucky, the Confederates enjoyed excellent railroad connections that gave them the distinct advantage of interior lines. They could reinforce any one region quickly by moving troops through these interior lines and a maze of tiny installations. To buoy this strength, Johnston's troops had built two forts on the Cumberland and Tennessee Rivers just below the Kentucky–Tennessee line. Fort Henry on the Tennessee River and Fort Donelson on the Cumberland River were designed to inhibit Federal navigation on these rivers.

While Halleck and Buell considered the best avenue by which to penetrate the South, Grant decided to head down the Mississippi River from Cairo, Illinois. On 7 November, some 3,000 troops were ferried downriver to Belmont, Missouri, opposite the bluffs of Columbus, Kentucky. Although Grant's troops moved swiftly to capture the tiny river hamlet, driving the defenders away, General Polk sent reinforcements across the river and soon forced Grant's troops to retreat. Aside from the casualties, which cost Confederates and Federals about 600 men each, Grant came to appreciate the strength of Columbus and the viability of using the Mississippi as an avenue of invasion south. Another route would have to open up.

Kentucky and Tennessee, winter and spring 1862

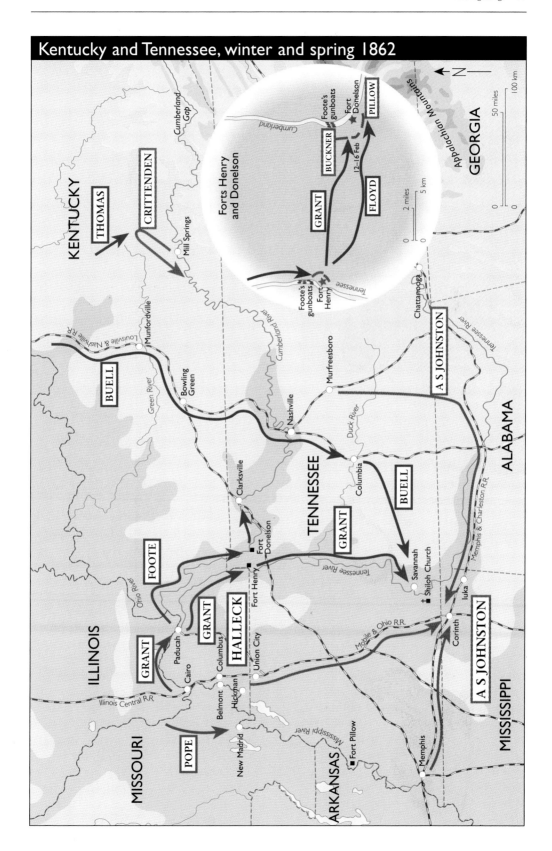

The campaign in Kentucky and Tennessee, 1861–62

As winter approached, the prospects of campaigning were dismal and the difficulty of moving men in the winter brought the Federal offensive to a halt. Both Union and Confederate armies went into winter quarters expecting little military activity, but commanders began to exploit the natural advantages afforded them by the rivers. In the months that followed, the Union's edge on the water helped it recover from the defeat at First Bull Run, Wilson's Creek, and Belmont. Union commanders pondered the best avenues of invasion. They could move down the Mississippi River against Columbus, which had proven to be impregnable; they could move by railroad from Louisville to Bowling Green into central Kentucky, which the Confederates could easily stall; or they could move up either the Tennessee or Cumberland River or both toward the river forts.

Whatever the case, the western commanders would first have to agree on the same avenue and, secondly, be willing to commit significant numbers of troops to hold on to supply areas as they moved south, which would reduce the number of troops for combat. A seemingly logical solution at the time, the divided departments would come to plague Union operations in the west, as neither Halleck nor Buell, cautious by nature and sensitive about administering their departments, could agree on the same route of invasion. Thus, the better part of the winter of 1861–62 was spent campaigning with a map. They convinced themselves that because the Confederates had the advantage of interior lines, any Union assault would have a distinct disadvantage. Consequently, an impatient Northern public and a frustrated president, tired of the inactivity, demanded an end to procrastination and the beginning of some movement in the west.

It was the subordinates of Halleck and Buell who, disheartened by the inactivity of camp life, convinced their superiors to allow them to take the initiative. The war began to

Commodore Andrew Foote was wounded by splinters of wood in his foot while on deck of the USS *St Louis*. Though somewhat incapacitated, he took part in the attack on Island No. 10 in April. His injury forced him to shore duty and in June he was transferred to Washington. (Ann Ronan Picture Library)

move in the west in early January when Halleck ordered Grant to send a small expeditionary force up the Tennessee River to test the defenses at Fort Henry. This diversionary trip, Halleck thought, might also force Johnston to consider his options as to where he might concentrate his force.

At the other end of the Confederate defensive line, Major-Generals George B. Crittenden and George H. Thomas engaged and defeated Confederate forces under Brigadier-General Felix Zollicoffer at the Battle of Mill Springs or Logan's Cross Roads, Kentucky. The battle, on 19 January 1862, revealed the weakness in Johnston's line and advanced the Union cause in the eastern portion of the Bluegrass state and in eastern Tennessee.

Meanwhile, Grant had finally convinced Halleck that Fort Henry could easily be taken. In early February about 15,000 troops boarded transports and steamed up the Tennessee. To cooperate with the Union troops, Grant ordered a flotilla of gunboats commanded by Flag Officer Andrew H. Foote to accompany the expedition. On 6 February, while Grant disembarked his troops, the flotilla continued upriver and at 11.00 am opened fire on the fort. Realizing that the Union forces were closing in by land and river, Brigadier-General Lloyd Tilghman decided to send the 2,500-man garrison out of the fort to Fort Donelson some 12 miles (19km) east. The winter rains had forced the Tennessee out of its banks and the fort had succumbed to nearly 6 feet (2m) of water. Within three hours, the gunboats had reduced the fort and forced Tilghman to surrender before Grant's infantrymen even arrived on the scene. 'Fort Henry is ours,' read the news as it made its way east. 'The flag of the Union is re-established on the soil of Tennessee,' asserted Halleck.

The Federals had correctly pinpointed the weakness in the Confederate defensive line: the Cumberland and Tennessee Rivers. Thinking that the Confederates would reinforce Fort Donelson on the Cumberland River, Grant destroyed the railroad over the Tennessee, sent gunboats south toward northern Alabama, and prepared to move eastward toward the river stronghold. Brigadier-General John B. Floyd commanded the Confederates at Fort Donelson, and Johnston decided to strengthen his line by sending some reinforcements, withdrawing part of the garrison at Columbus and abandoning Bowling Green. Confederate authorities had faced the crucial dilemma that would plague them for the rest of the war: how and where to defend the several-hundred-mile line with insufficient forces at their disposal.

Although reinforcing the fort seemed the strategic thing to do, it ultimately proved to be a colossal mistake. On 13 February, Grant's army of 23,000 men had made it to Fort Donelson and encircled it. The following day, Foote's gunboats arrived and began shelling the fort from the river, expecting to force its surrender. After several

Ulysses S. Grant seized Fort Donelson and with it considerable fame. When he was asked for terms after defeating a Confederate breakout attempt, his reply earned him the nickname 'Unconditional Surrender' Grant. (Ann Ronan Picture Library)

hours of heavy shelling, however, the fort's well-positioned artillery forced the gunboats to retire. The cold and blustery day ended and the two disheartened armies prepared to do battle the next day. During the night, the Confederate command, convinced that Grant had completely invested the fort by now, determined to attempt a breakout and head south. The next day, 15 February, General Pillow, aided by some of General Buckner's men, broke through the Federal line after a brutal fight. When nothing was done to break the entire army out of the fort, Floyd ordered his army to return to their fortifications.

That evening the Confederates held a council of war and determined to surrender. Floyd and Pillow abdicated their responsibility as the highest-ranking commanders and left the job to General Buckner, a prewar friend of Grant's. When Buckner requested terms of surrender on 16 February, Grant replied, 'No terms except unconditional and immediate surrender can be accepted.' The words that forever immortalized him as 'Unconditional Surrender' Grant gave the Union its first real victory of the entire war.

Strategically, the loss of the river forts was catastrophic to the Confederacy, but equally significant was the fact that Grant also captured the reinforcements sent to support the garrison. Some 12,500 soldiers and 40 guns were surrendered. The next day, the Northern press printed a sensational story of the Donelson campaign, made Grant an unsuspecting hero, but gave Halleck credit for planning the entire invasion. Frustrated by the news that 'All was quiet along the Potomac,' all winter, Lincoln was elated by the news along the Tennessee and Cumberland Rivers and instantly rewarded

the nation's new hero with a promotion to major-general of volunteers.

The Union invasion along the rivers forced the Confederates to retreat south all the way to the Tennessee–Mississippi and Alabama border. Northern gunboats now threatened Southern river towns as far south as Clarksville and Nashville. Columbus, a Confederate stronghold on the Mississippi, also succumbed to the Federals, as did a significant portion of Middle Tennessee. Tennessee Governor Isham Harris prepared to abandon Nashville and move the government with him to Memphis. Significantly, the rivers, the great market highways that had provided a regional unity at harvest times, had now become the axis of military invasion and the great weakness of the Confederacy during the winter.

On the heels of the defeats in the west, there was a somber mood in Richmond on 22 February, the day Jefferson Davis was inaugurated President of the Confederacy. As the rain poured, the Confederate President claimed that 'The tyranny of the unbridled majority, the most odious and least responsible form of despotism, has denied us both the right and the remedy. Therefore we are in arms to renew such sacrifices as our fathers made to the holy cause of constitutional liberty.' While he was speaking, the citizens and soldiers of Nashville were evacuating the city. By the 25th, the Tennessee capital had surrendered to Union commander Don Carlos Buell. Wanting to move quickly to restore civilian government to the occupied region, Lincoln had named Andrew Johnson military governor of the state.

Confederate Commander Simon Bolivar Buckner was a prewar friend of Grant and had loaned him money. When John B. Floyd and Gideon Pillow abdicated responsibility for surrendering Fort Donelson, Buckner yielded to circumstances and accepted Grant's unfriendly terms of 'Unconditional Surrender.' (Ann Ronan Picture Library)

West of the Mississippi River, Major-General John Pope assumed command of the Army of the Mississippi at Commerce, Missouri. He ordered his troops to move against New Madrid, Missouri, in an attempt to dislodge the Confederate stronghold at Island No. 10 near the Kentucky–Tennessee border. By the time the Confederates had evacuated Columbus, Kentucky, Federal troops under Brigadier-General Samuel R. Curtis had pushed the Confederates under Major-General Sterling Price south out of Missouri and into the northwestern portion of Arkansas. At Fayetteville, Confederate General Earl Van Dorn joined Price in an

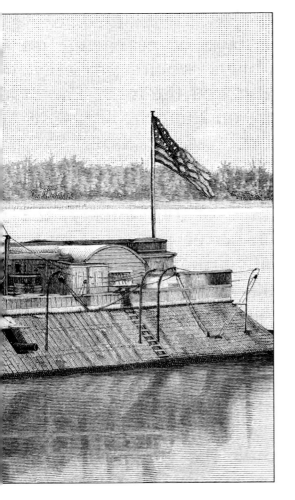

The *St Louis* was one of the earliest ironclad gunboats constructed. It saw action against Confederate batteries at Columbus, Kentucky, Fort Henry, Fort Donelson, and Memphis. In October 1862, its name changed to *Baron de Kalb* and it participated in river action against Vicksburg in 1862–63. A Confederate torpedo sank the ironclad on 12 July 1863, in the Yazoo River. (Ann Ronan Picture Library)

Known as the 'Hero of Fort Sumter,' Pierre Gustav Beauregard was second in command to Albert Sidney Johnston, who commanded the Army of Mississippi. After Johnston was killed at the Battle of Shiloh, 6–7 April 1862, Beauregard assumed command of the army, but he was relieved by Jefferson Davis shortly after. (Ann Ronan Picture Library)

before heading south. Confident that the Confederates would not attack, Grant assembled his army at Pittsburg Landing, a well-known landing for river transports. It was about 25 miles (40km) north of Corinth, and above the river bluffs the land was relatively flat, which made the landing a suitable choice to land a large number of troops. Still, it was on the west side of the Tennessee River and Halleck had ordered Grant to await reinforcements from Buell's army before heading south toward Corinth. Buell had departed Nashville with 36,000 men and was expected to meet up with Grant before he crossed his army over the river.

effort to stop the Federal advance, and on 7–8 March they counterattacked at the Battle of Pea Ridge. The Union victory allowed Halleck to concentrate his energies east of the Mississippi.

Having assumed command of the entire west, Halleck ordered his armies south to occupy Corinth, Mississippi, an important railroad junction on the Memphis and Charleston, or the 'Vertebrae of the Confederacy,' as the Confederate Secretary of War, Leroy P. Walker, characterized it. The Mobile and Ohio line bisected the Memphis and Charleston at Corinth, and Halleck came to believe that after Richmond, occupation of this tiny railway junction might bring the rebellion to a close.

Halleck ordered Grant to Savannah, Tennessee, to wait for Buell to reinforce him

The Battle of Shiloh

After a bleak winter that had proved tremendously unsettling to the Southern cause, spring 1862 brought hope that the Confederates in the west might redeem their losses. Johnston concentrated his defeated forces near Corinth, Mississippi, for an offensive into Tennessee. He had pleaded all winter for reinforcements, but none were forthcoming until March, when he was able to muster some 40,000 troops to engage the enemy. Realizing that the Federals possessed superior numerical strength, the Confederates would have to pull off a stunning surprise and run Grant's army into the river before Buell arrived if they were to be successful. The concentration of forces brought together a colorful group of commanders, including Major-Generals Braxton Bragg and Pierre G. T. Beauregard, the hero of the Battle of First Bull Run. Johnston assumed overall command.

In Hebrew, Shiloh translates as 'Place of Peace.' It is an ironic name given to a church near Pittsburg Landing, Tennessee, the scene of the most fiercely contested battle of the war in the Western Theater. Shiloh church was located in the middle of the Battle of Shiloh. It proved the inspiration for the noted author Herman Melville to compose an elegiac memorial to those who perished beside the humble country church. In 'Shiloh: A Requiem,' Melville attempted with poetic words to return Shiloh church to the quiet refuge it had once been. (*Harper's Weekly*)

The Battle of Shiloh, 6–7 April 1862

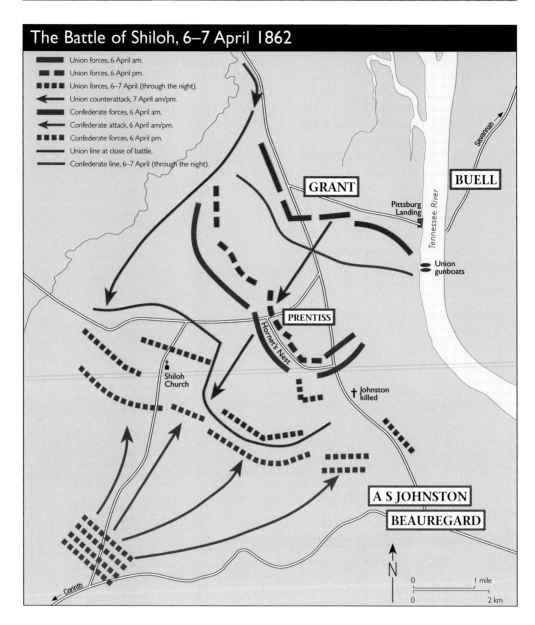

Union forces, 6 April am.
Union forces, 6 April pm.
Union forces, 6–7 April (through the night).
Union counterattack, 7 April am/pm.
Confederate forces, 6 April am.
Confederate attack, 6 April am/pm.
Confederate forces, 6 April pm.
Union line at close of battle.
Confederate line, 6–7 April (through the night).

GRANT

BUELL

Pittsburg
Landing

Tennessee River

Savannah →

Union
gunboats

PRENTISS

Horner's Nest

Shiloh
Church

Johnston
killed

A S JOHNSTON

BEAUREGARD

N

Corinth

0   1 mile
0   2 km

The largely unseasoned Confederate Army of the Mississippi left Corinth on 3 April. Muddy roads and the inhospitable terrain, however, stalled the advance for two days, forcing Beauregard to conclude that the element of surprise had been lost. Nonsense, Johnston remarked on the evening of 5 April, 'I would fight them if they were a million.' The same evening Buell had made it to Savannah, a few miles downriver from Pittsburg Landing. The countryside around Pittsburg Landing was cut by ravines,

blanketed by heavy underbrush and blossoming peach trees, and crossed by a maze of small creeks and old wagon trails that bisected one another. The only distinguishing landmark was a small Methodist church that stood near the main road to Corinth. The church was known as Shiloh, which in Hebrew means 'Place of Peace.'

It was early on Palm Sunday, 6 April, when a Union patrol ventured out toward the woods and detected a wave of

Confederates, who fired an enormous volley, opening the Battle of Pittsburg Landing. To the Federals' surprise, the Confederates had struck at dawn. Major-General William T. Sherman, who had insisted that the enemy was no closer than Corinth, commanded the Federals near the church and was forced to form a line to hold off the Confederate wave. The Confederates thrust forward throughout the early morning hours, pushing the panic-stricken soldiers back toward the river. Although somewhat oddly formed and badly intermingled in its deployment, the Confederate offensive was nonetheless so successful that by noon thousands of the disorganized Federals had simply run for cover, some cowering beneath the river bluff, others swimming across the river for safety. Still, most of the Federal troops remained steadfast and throughout the morning both sides engaged in a horrific slaughter.

When Grant arrived on the grisly scene it was about 8.30 am. He pulled stragglers together to form a defensive line and left word at Savannah for Buell to get his troops across the river. In the meantime, Grant had

to hold on. As the Confederates continued to push the Federals back, they ran into a stubborn resistance in the center. Brigadier-General Benjamin Prentiss's division was located in a densely wooded area with open fields on both sides and an old sunken wagon trail in its front that provided an entrenchment. Grant ordered Prentiss to hold his position at all costs – an order that he obeyed throughout the day. Because of the intensity of the fight in this location, soldiers later dubbed this portion of the battlefield the 'Hornet's Nest.'

All day long, Johnston's Confederates tried in vain to envelop and dislodge the Federals. Although the Federals were running low on ammunition, they still repulsed wave after wave of Confederate assaults. At one point Johnston himself led one of the

These riverboats provided much needed assistance for the Union army at the Battle of Shiloh in April 1862. Grant made his headquarters aboard the *Tigress*, the middle vessel of the three. It was aboard this steamer that Buell and Grant met briefly to discuss the strategy that brought ultimate victory on the second day of the battle. (Review of Reviews Company)

charges and was mortally wounded. He bled to death while his personal physician was helping to care for captured wounded Federals. After several futile and suicidal bayonet charges, the Confederates positioned over 60 cannon in a semicircle to rain down several hundred shells on the Union stronghold. Practically surrounded, Prentiss reluctantly surrendered at 5.30 pm to save the 2,200 men left in his division. During the remaining hour of daylight, Grant struggled to reposition his artillery to hold off the anticipated final Confederate thrust. As darkness came, so did the rains, and the merciless fighting ended.

Now in command of the victorious Confederate forces, Beauregard concluded that the Federals would retreat during the night, so he did not position his scattered and disorganized forces to receive an offensive. Instead, he waited for Van Dorn to arrive from Arkansas. Buell was reportedly too far away to reinforce Grant. But the night rains and darkness favored the Union

army. Although both sides were exhausted, Buell had, in fact, arrived and the four divisions that crossed the river numbered some 28,000 men, who were anxious to fight. Although it had been a rough day, Grant had been significantly reinforced and he would assume the offensive the following morning. As he walked the lines during the night, he came across a fatigued General Sherman, who had been in the thick of the fighting all day. Sherman suggested that it had been a horrific fight; Grant agreed, but remarked, 'Whip 'em tomorrow, though.'

Early the following morning, the Federals stunned the unsuspecting Confederates with an overwhelming counteroffensive. Throughout the morning and early afternoon, the soldiers fought over the same terrain, scattered with wounded and dead soldiers and horses, and half-submerged artillery pieces sunken by the rain. Like the previous day, the combat was severe and bloody. From the river, Union gunboats lobbed scores of shells down on the

Southern combatants. When Beauregard realized that Van Dorn was not coming, and that his troops were nearly out of ammunition and completely exhausted, he ordered a withdrawal to Corinth. Grant decided not to pursue because his soldiers were just as exhausted and disorganized as the retreating troops.

Although the Union won the battle, both sides lost overwhelming numbers of casualties. Union casualties totaled over 13,000, while the Confederates lost over 10,000. Never before was the American populace confronted by such staggering news as the losses at Shiloh. Northerners came to believe that the human toll far exceeded the strategic gains in the west and that something must have gone seriously wrong. Although the Federals had extinguished Confederate hopes for reclaiming West Tennessee and stalled the Union penetration of significant cotton-producing regions in Mississippi and Alabama, Northern politicians were pressed for answers about the high casualty rate. As rumors passed through the Federal camps that the Confederates had surprised Grant, that he had been drinking, and that he had not even been on the field when the battle opened, Lincoln and Halleck were forced to defend the commander. At one point, frustrated about the failures and inactivity in the east, Lincoln supposedly defended Grant, arguing that although he might be the cause of the losses at Shiloh, 'I can't spare this man; he fights.'

The same day that Grant and Buell defeated Beauregard, General Pope captured Island No. 10, which opened the Mississippi River all the way to Memphis, Tennessee. In the following weeks, the Union Navy steamed down the Mississippi toward Memphis, and Halleck came to Pittsburg Landing to direct the combined Federal armies of Grant and Buell against Corinth.

Confederate gunboats burning at New Orleans on the approach of the Federal fleets. (Public domain)

Perhaps even more stunning than the Union victory at Shiloh was Flag Officer David G. Farragut's capture of New Orleans, Louisiana, three weeks later. His wooden frigates and gunboats, carrying Brigadier-General Benjamin Butler's 15,000 soldiers, approached the forts protecting the mouth of the Mississippi River. After a week of bombarding the strongholds, Farragut's mortars failed to reduce the forts, so the determined sailor decided to run his flotilla by the forts. Before daybreak on 24 April, Farragut slipped his 17 vessels past the forts and moved upriver, though the Confederates managed to disable three smaller vessels. Less than a week later, Farragut's sailors and marines captured New Orleans without resistance as Brigadier-General Mansfield Lovell sent his forces away from the city. Simultaneously, General Butler forced the surrender of the river forts and then sent his men to occupy New Orleans.

Not only had the Federals captured the Confederacy's largest city and leading port, but also the capture came on the heels of the defeat at Shiloh. Again the Confederates suffered the consequences of a lack of manpower to cover the vast western terrain. Confederate authorities believed that the main Union offensive was to come from upriver, so they ordered most of the soldiers and several gunboats north, leaving New Orleans vulnerable to attack.

The cumulative effect of these disasters was devastating to the Confederacy. The loss of Forts Henry and Donelson, the bloody defeat at Shiloh, and the capture of two of the Confederacy's most prominent cities, Nashville and New Orleans, cast a dark shadow over the war effort. The loss of these strategic places and manpower, coupled with the fact that McClellan had besieged Yorktown, Virginia, and was preparing to advance against Richmond with the largest force ever assembled on the North American continent, forced the Confederate government to consider desperate measures. On 16 April, the Confederate Congress approved the first National Conscription Act in the nation's history. Although some

Confederates bitterly opposed this Act, arguing that it was an infringement of their liberties, others argued that the Confederacy with its limited manpower must raise troops and that states' rights would have to succumb to the Confederate cause. All white males between 18 and 35 years of age would be subjected to three years' military service.

As the victory bells rang throughout the North in celebration of the accomplishments in the west, Southerners had no such expression. In fact, in stark contrast, church bells and plantation bells in the South were being melted down to be used in the war effort. At one point, Beauregard wrote to Father James Mullen of St Patrick's church in New Orleans that although 'our wives and children have been accustomed to the call, and would miss the tones of the "Church-going bells," … there is no alternative we must make the sacrifice …' As much as he wanted to spare the necessity of depriving the South's plantations and churches of their bells, he simply could not. The war was heating up and Beauregard needed every available resource to carry on his operations to restore the Confederacy in the west.

Union advances into Mississippi and Tennessee

After Shiloh and the capture of New Orleans, the pace of Union success slowed, but Federal armies were still on the move. By the end of May 1862, Halleck's enormous army of over 100,000 troops had cautiously inched its way to Corinth, Mississippi, thinking that the Confederates had regrouped and would give battle. Beauregard, however, was in no position to fight Halleck and deceptively evacuated the small rail town during the night of 29 May, heading south to Tupelo, Mississippi, some 80 miles (130km) away. In one of the great ruses of the war, the entire operation was carried out so skillfully that Halleck and his commanders were oblivious.

When Halleck rode into Corinth on the afternoon of 30 May, he found an empty town. At one point he noticed a blue uniform stuffed with straw hanging by the neck from a scrubby tree limb. Nearby a pine board was nailed fast, and on it was written 'Halleck outwitted – what will old Abe say?' Nonetheless, Halleck claimed that the capture of Corinth the following day was as 'brilliant and important a victory as any recorded in history.' Lincoln was impressed.

The Union's capture of Corinth broke the Memphis and Charleston railroad and disabled the Confederates' east–west link. Memphis, Tennessee, was now vulnerable to Union gunboats on the river and foot soldiers from the east, who pushed their way toward the city. As thousands of people lined the river bluffs early on the morning of 6 June to witness what they believed would be the final river fight, Commodore Charles Davis steamed downriver and opened the fight. After two hours of furious gunboat warfare, the fighting ended at 7.30 am. The Federals had completely destroyed the Confederates and a few hours later the mayor surrendered the city. With Memphis in Union hands, the Federals could use it as a supply base as they moved downriver. The Mississippi was now open all the way to Vicksburg, Mississippi, considered

This portrait of William T. Sherman conveys the image of the Union general as described by a contemporary, who wrote that Sherman was 'the most American looking man I ever saw, tall and lank, not very erect, with hair like thatch.' (Ann Ronan Picture Library)

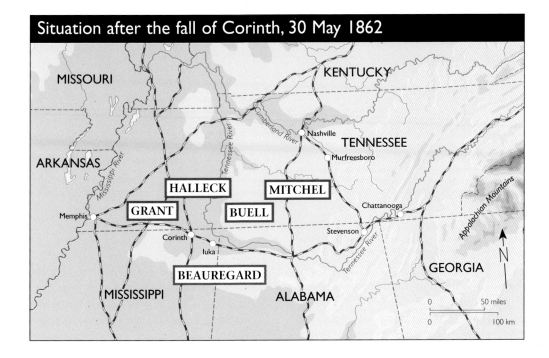

Situation after the fall of Corinth, 30 May 1862

by Confederates to be the 'Gibraltar of the West.'

By June 1862, no commander in either army could boast of successes like Halleck's in the Western Theater of war. With Kentucky, Missouri, Tennessee, and much of Arkansas in Federal hands, 'Old Brains', as Halleck was commonly known before the war (an inference due to the size of his forehead and his intellect), had become the architect of success. Northern hopes for an end to the war escalated. But as the rivers began to shrink due to the summer heat, so too did Union activity in the west begin to decelerate.

Waging a limited war for limited goals, at a time when Union armies were now poised to strike at the South's vital slavery districts in the west, proved cumbersome for Union commanders whose armies occupied a region

On the morning of 6 June 1862, thousands of residents lined the river bluffs to view the Battle of Memphis. It took less than two hours for the Union fleet to reduce the city, and the Union used the Mississippi River city as a base for the Vicksburg expedition. (Ann Ronan Picture Library)

about the size of France. Fighting in battle constituted one brand of warfare, but attempting to maintain supremacy in the occupied regions while respecting the constitutional rights of Southern civilians, including their right to own slaves, would soon demoralize soldiers and Northern civilians alike. Thus the summer of 1862 was a defining period not so much in combat, but rather in how far Union authorities and the Union populace would go in continuing to support Lincoln's desire to fight a war that made ultimate peace and reunion possible.

By mid-June, with the rivers no longer at his disposal, Halleck had dispersed his large army overland and turned his sights to securing the fruits of his army's labors. He ordered Buell and his 31,000 soldiers east toward Chattanooga, an important Tennessee city on the edge of the Appalachians, through which passed the Memphis and Charleston railroad and the Tennessee River. Because his army would be marching in the same direction as the railroad, Halleck considered the use of the iron horse to be an asset to Buell's campaign. But the railroad in this case proved to be a curse, and Buell's army would have serious difficulty in moving east. In the meantime, Halleck used Grant and Sherman to police West Tennessee with the 67,000 soldiers left in his grand army. The string of victories ceased.

By mid-July, Lincoln had made Halleck his chief-of-staff, which left Grant the command in West Tennessee and Buell the command of his soldiers stalled in northern Alabama. Because of the disposition of their forces, neither commander was prepared to continue the momentum of offensive warfare. The recalcitrant temper of the Southern populace, guerrilla activity, and the frustration of protecting long and vulnerable supply lines and railroads all combined to stall operations.

The Confederate counteroffensive

During the summer of 1862, in the absence of offensive Union strikes, the Confederates seized the opportunity to take the war back into the Upper South states of Tennessee and Kentucky. Besides, the Federals had held the upper hand long enough in those states that civilians might desire Confederate redemption, particularly in light of the fact that Northern authorities were directing their armies to strike at the institution of slavery. About the same time that Halleck left the west, so too did Beauregard. Major-General Braxton Bragg was his successor.

Confederate General Braxton Bragg had a distinguished prewar career. After serving in the Seminole War, Bragg won three brevets in the Mexican War. He was ordered to command in the west in early 1862 and participated in the battles of Shiloh, Perryville, Stone's River, Chickamauga, and Chattanooga. He was constantly in dispute with several top commanders, which considerably weakened his command. (Ann Ronan Picture Library)

A West Point graduate and Mexican War veteran, Bragg enjoyed a prominent reputation. He was bright, industrious, and an able administrator, but his argumentative manner often invited criticism and alienated him from others. Still, once he assumed command of the Confederate army in the west, he was determined to redeem the Confederacy's lost fortunes. Having been driven from the Confederate heartland, Bragg devised a scheme that would reverse the war in the west.

Bragg's Kentucky invasion began after the Confederates retreated south to Tupelo in June. From there he would move his 22,500-man army by rail to Mobile and then to Chattanooga before Buell reached the city. In mid-July, he left Van Dorn at Tupelo and set out on a circuitous journey that would take several weeks, finally reaching Chattanooga by the end of August. From

The Western Theater, summer–fall, 1862

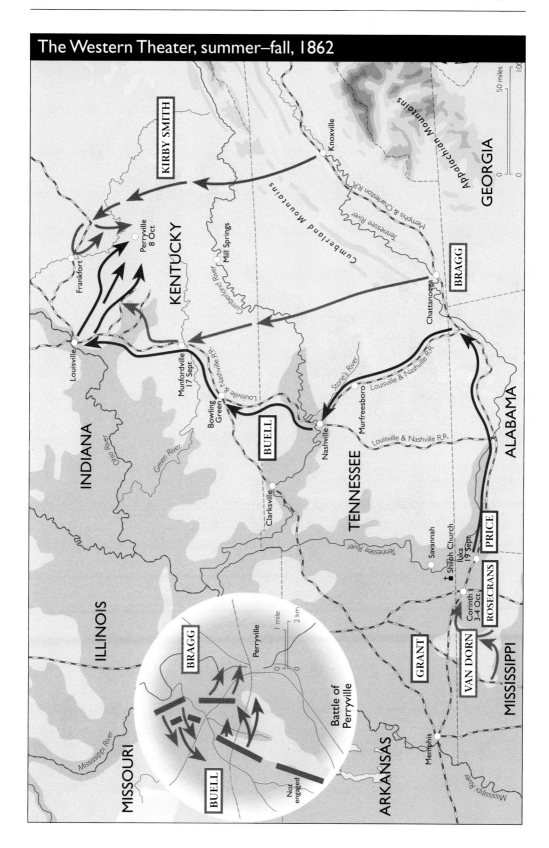

Battle of Perryville

there he and Major-General Edmund Kirby Smith, already at Lexington, Kentucky, with 10,000 soldiers, would bypass Nashville and head north to Louisville. Along the way he was disappointed to find that Kentuckians showed little interest in enlisting in his Confederate ranks, as he had hoped. Nearing Louisville, Bragg's forces captured Munfordville on 17 September after convincing the Federal commander there, Colonel John T. Wilder, that he was greatly outnumbered. Residents of Louisville and across the Ohio River were panic-stricken that Bragg's army would soon arrive and advance across the river into Indiana.

Bragg's raid into Kentucky forced Buell to abandon northern Alabama and return to Louisville to protect the city. Consequently, he forfeited much of the region that his army had fought hard to conquer earlier in the year. Though it was a demoralizing march, to its credit his army moved swiftly north, some days marching nearly 30 miles (48km), and by the end of September had made it to Louisville.

In early October, Buell's 60,000 men engaged Bragg's force of less than half that size at the Battle of Perryville. The battle opened on the 8th when soldiers from both armies, searching for water, blundered into one another. The fight developed chaotically, as neither commander fully understood the strength or exact whereabouts of the other commander's entire army. In Buell's case, peculiar atmospheric conditions prevented him from realizing the seriousness of the engagement until the afternoon. By 2.00 pm the battle was raging furiously, although Buell was unable to commit his entire army to the fight. By nightfall, the uncoordinated character of the battle yielded little of immediate significance, except that the Federals had lost roughly 4,200 casualties and the Confederates about 3,400 men.

Though both commanders interpreted the fight to be a victory on their part, Bragg recognized during the night that Buell outnumbered him and would make short work of the Confederates unless he abandoned the battlefield and retreated

Confederate General Earl Van Dorn was sent to command in Arkansas early in 1862. His army lost the Battle of Pea Ridge in March 1862, and was shortly after ordered east of the Mississippi River. In 1862, he successfully defended Vicksburg, but in October he failed to retake Corinth, Mississippi, and was shortly after ordered to serve under John C. Pemberton. (Review of Reviews Company)

south. His invasion of Kentucky was over and in the days following the battle he crossed back into Tennessee and encamped at Murfreesboro. When Buell made excuses for not pursuing Bragg, Lincoln lost his patience with the overly cautious commander and eliminated him from command.

The initial Confederate late-summer thrusts to counter the Union spring offensive ended in October. By the time Bragg and Buell finally met at Perryville, other battles had taken place in northern Mississippi. At Iuka, just a few miles southeast of Corinth, General Grant sent Major-General William S. Rosecrans with 15,000 soldiers to dislodge Sterling Price's Confederates. On 19 September, Rosecrans succeeded in driving Price away before he could be reinforced by Earl Van Dorn at Tupelo and move into West Tennessee. In the weeks that followed, however, Van Dorn arrived to reinforce Price. Together the Confederates advanced to Corinth and battled Rosecrans for two days, on 3–4 October, but failed to defeat him. Fresh from victory, Rosecrans replaced Buell.

With Price and Van Dorn checked by Grant's forces in northern Mississippi, and now with Bragg retiring back to Tennessee, the Confederates would never again be poised to redeem either Kentucky or

Northern-born John C. Pemberton resigned his commission in 1861 to offer his services in the Confederate army. In 1862, he was promoted to lieutenant-general and sent to guard Vicksburg and Port Hudson on the Mississippi River. By the summer of 1863, the Union army had enveloped his command, forcing it into Vicksburg. The Federals laid siege to the town, forcing it to capitulate on 4 July. (Ann Ronan Picture Library)

Tennessee. The Southern populace would have more to worry about than the sacrifice of their plantations and church bells. The Union army was bearing down on the South's wealthiest cotton and agricultural regions, where slaves were most numerous.

The Vicksburg campaign

Having survived the Confederate attack at Corinth, Grant now focused his attention on the Mississippi River citadel of Vicksburg, located 300 miles (480km) south of Memphis on a hairpin turn high above the river. The city's small size, however, belied its military importance. Not only was it a prosperous and strategically significant city linked by

rail; it was also the link between the Confederate forces east and west of the river. If Vicksburg were captured, the Confederacy would have no chance to coordinate operations in the region or move supplies from Texas to the east. Throughout the spring and summer the Union had failed to capture the city. But with renewed vigor, Grant decided to direct a more concerted effort to achieve that objective.

In November 1862, Grant's army, now designated the Army of the Tennessee, set out overland south on a 250-mile (400km) journey. It would require quartermasters to perform herculean labors to keep his 40,000 soldiers fed by using the north–south Mississippi Central railroad. The inhospitable geography of the Yazoo Delta country, characterized by swamps and vast stretches of woodlands without roads, made for frustrating campaigning. Grant had concluded that the only feasible way to reduce the risk to his army and to be in a position to capture the city once the army arrived would be to move slowly, but steadily.

Lieutenant-General John C. Pemberton was the Confederate commander assigned to defend Vicksburg. As Grant advanced south, Pemberton retreated in the face of numerical superiority all the way to Grenada, Mississippi. To strengthen his chances, Grant divided his army into two movements on Vicksburg in early December. He ordered Sherman to return to Memphis with a division, collect enough troops to give him more than 20,000 men, and move down the Mississippi River with Admiral David Dixon Porter's gunboats. The amphibious expedition was designed to strike at Vicksburg from one direction while Grant advanced from central Mississippi, hoping to paralyze Pemberton.

Grant advanced all the way to Oxford, Mississippi, and Sherman had made it to Vicksburg by the time Nathan Bedford Forrest's Confederate cavalrymen had destroyed numerous stretches of the railroad. Earl Van Dorn meanwhile raided Grant's supply base at Holly Springs, Mississippi,

capturing 1,500 Federals and destroying $1,500,000 worth of supplies. With his communications severed and his principal supply depot wrecked, Grant pulled back, enabling Pemberton to swing a portion of his army at Sherman. On 29 December, the Confederates managed to repel both Union forces.

Forced to live off the countryside in mid-December, Federal troops stripped the landscape bare of livestock, grain, and forage. When the inhabitants begged for enough to live on through the winter, Grant sternly ordered them to move further south. It was a dismal winter, although the Federals managed to suffer less than the Southerners.

The Battle of Stone's River

Some 300 miles (480km) northeast of Vicksburg, Rosecrans replaced Buell in late October 1862. The army became known once again as the Army of the Cumberland. Rosecrans's nickname, 'Old Rosy,' was an accurate characterization of his temper. Red-cheeked, affable, and energetic, Rosecrans was a favorite among the soldiers. Slovenliness infuriated him and he impressed soldiers by purging his command of incompetents. 'Everything for the service, nothing for individuals,' was his motto. Still, he was cautious and wavered at the critical hour.

When he inherited the army it was in Nashville, where he spent nearly two months preparing to move against Bragg's 38,000-man army, encamped at Murfreesboro along a swollen Stone's River. On 26 December, he set out with his 47,000 men to hit Bragg. Having been abused by the press and feeling political pressure for abandoning Kentucky, Bragg was determined not to be defeated. To the east of Stone's River he positioned Major-General John C. Breckinridge, and to the west of the river Bragg deployed his main force. By 29 December, Rosecrans's army had arrived in the vicinity of Murfreesboro, and during the night he positioned his men along the

Union General William S. Rosecrans was sent west at his own request and
served under John Pope during the advance on Corinth, Mississippi, in May 1862.
He fought successfully at the Battle of Corinth in October, and replaced Don
Carlos Buell in November. Well liked by his men and a brilliant strategist,
Rosecrans was known for his heavy drinking, profuse language, and hot temper,
and his soldiers dubbed him 'Old Rosey'. (Hulton Getty)

Nashville turnpike several hundred yards from the Confederate line.

Ironically, both Rosecrans and Bragg had determined to attack the enemy's left flank, which meant that whoever attacked first would be advantaged. Bragg awaited an attack throughout the day on 30 December, but none was forthcoming. Bragg then struck the first blow on the following day by marching Major-General William Hardee's corps around the Federal right flank. At dawn, Hardee's men surprised the Federals and drove them back toward the Murfreesboro–Nashville turnpike and pinned them against Stone's River. The Confederates threw brigade after brigade at the Federal line, but failed to break it as both Generals George H. Thomas and Philip H. Sheridan resisted stubbornly.

As the early sunset, the last of 1862, closed the day's fighting, Bragg believed he had won a major victory. Indeed, he had redeemed his army's fortunes. 'God has granted us a Happy New Year,' he telegraphed Richmond. That night Rosecrans held a council of war and questioned his corps commanders as to the feasibility of a retreat. 'Hell,' Thomas replied, 'this army can't retreat.' Impressed by the resolve of his subordinates, Rosecrans decided to stay and fight.

The new year opened quietly and ominously. It was cold and the soldiers were tense with anticipation. They had recovered from the previous day's fight and were expecting any minute to commence fighting again. But the fighting never came. Rosecrans redeployed his troops to strengthen his lines, while Confederate scouts concluded that this was a ruse to mask the Federal retreat. On

This sketch by an artist of *Frank Leslie's Illustrated* depicts the Battle of Stone's River. On Friday, 2 January 1863, at about 4.00 pm, General Rosecrans ordered a final charge of General James Negley's Union division across Stone's River. Here the 18th Ohio Infantry, followed close behind by the 19th Illinois and the 21st Ohio, made their way across the river. The artist of this sketch reported that 'the scene was grand in the extreme. It was indeed a momentous battle on a miniature scale.' (Ann Ronan Picture Library)

2 January 1863, Bragg was dumbfounded to find that Rosecrans had not left. When the Confederate commander ordered Breckinridge to dislodge what he thought remained of the enemy force east of Stone's River late in the afternoon, the Federals initially fell back. As the Confederates advanced to the river, they found to their tremendous surprise that the Federals had prepared to counter the charge. Nearly 60 Federal cannon unleashed a thunderous barrage, and a counter of infantrymen followed that retired the Confederates in short order.

With his army exhausted and convinced that Rosecrans had been reinforced, Bragg reluctantly left the battlefield that night. He fell back to Tullahoma, Tennessee, thus conceding the battlefield and the victory to Rosecrans, whose soldiers had stood their ground. The Battle of Stone's River was a stalemate that cost the Union some 13,000 casualties and the Confederates roughly 10,200 casualties, or in both cases roughly 30 percent of their forces. In proportion to

men engaged and men lost, this battle ranked as the bloodiest of all battles.

The Union campaign on the Mississippi

Southern hopes of redeeming the western losses had been significantly dashed by the new year. The Union army was now poised to move against Chattanooga. One demoralized Confederate remarked, 'I am sick and tired of this war, and I can see no prospects of having peace for a long time to come, I don't think it ever will be stopped by fighting, the Yankees can't whip us and we can never whip them.' Lincoln was so impressed by the victory that he later confided to Rosecrans, 'you gave us a hard earned victory which, had there been a defeat instead, the nation could hardly have lived over.'

The Civil War had not begun with Union authorities arguing that points of occupation were more important than defeating Confederate armies. By 1863, however, it certainly appeared that this was the case in the Western Theater. The war in this region was about occupation of significant Southern ports, railroad junctions, cities, loyalist pockets, and plantation districts. Although this meant supplying armies over long distances and protecting the vital transportation arteries, the Union held firm to a belief that occupying strategic points would ultimately bring about the demise of the Confederacy. It was how to conduct affairs as proprietors of Southern domain rather than how to combat soldiers that consumed the attention of Union authorities. The resolve of Southern soldiers and civilians alike convinced many commanders that the war would not end until popular support ended. Consequently, the limited-war attitude gave way to total war – the seizure and destruction of personal property as part of subjugating the enemy, irrespective of their presumed loyalty.

The Union campaigns of 1863, therefore, would be at a distinct advantage over those

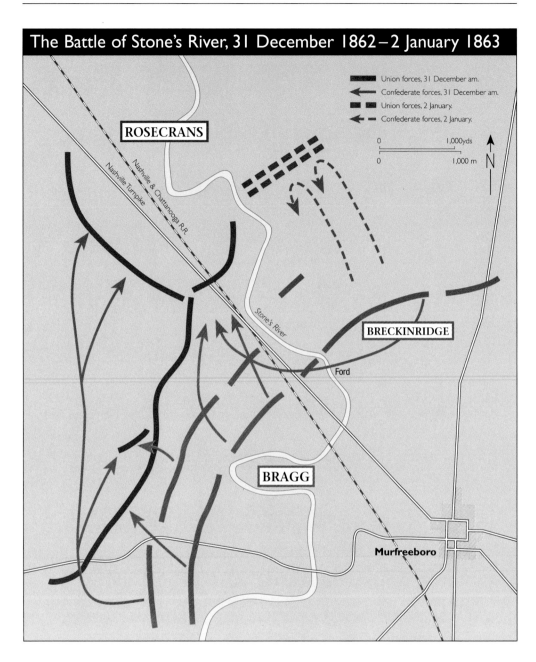

The Battle of Stone's River, 31 December 1862 – 2 January 1863

Union forces, 31 December am.
Confederate forces, 31 December am.
Union forces, 2 January.
Confederate forces, 2 January.

ROSECRANS

Nashville Turnpike

Nashville & Chattanooga R.R.

Stone's River

BRECKINRIDGE

Ford

BRAGG

Murfreeboro

of the previous year. Commanders were able to exercise more liberality in foraging, confiscating contraband, and dealing with Southern civilians. Still, the objects remained the same. Control of the Mississippi River was paramount to the Union's strategic plan in the west. Although Confederates considered the Memphis and Charleston the backbone of their nation, Federals came to believe that the great spinal cord of the

Confederacy was the Mississippi. The Confederates still held two vital points on the river: Port Hudson, Louisiana, 25 miles (40km) north of Baton Rouge, and Vicksburg, near the mouth of the Yazoo River. But because they never managed to develop sufficient naval strength, Confederates were unable to control the river that they claimed for the Confederacy. Meanwhile, because of the river campaigns of early 1862, Union

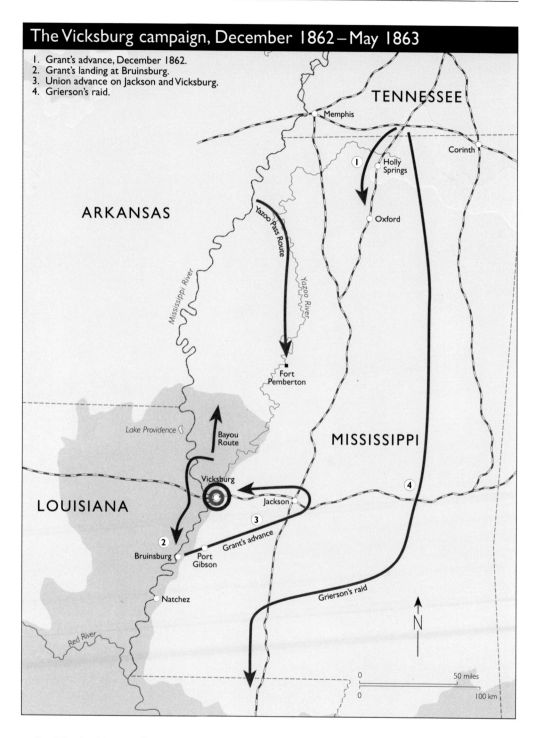

The Vicksburg campaign, December 1862 – May 1863

1. Grant's advance, December 1862.
2. Grant's landing at Bruinsburg.
3. Union advance on Jackson and Vicksburg.
4. Grierson's raid.

authorities had invested in new boats specifically designed for river warfare.

Nothing of much consequence occurred in January, as winter storms inhibited military operations. On 2 February, in broad winter daylight, the Union ram *Queen of the West* steamed past the Vicksburg batteries. Although it was struck 12 times, its commander, Colonel Charles R. Ellet, made it past and then struck three Confederate vessels, destroying the

By February, Grant's army had taken up winter camp at Milliken's Bend, a few miles north of Vicksburg, where he devised a series of plans to take the river fortress. The difficulty of getting his army into a position to successfully attack the city remained his nemesis. Throughout the winter and early spring, he attempted a number of schemes. He put his soldiers to work constructing a complex makeshift waterway by connecting creeks, old river channels, and bayous,

A Confederate siege-gun mounted in the river fortifications at Port Hudson, Louisiana. The Confederates blasted 20 of these pieces with deadly precision at David Farragut's fleet throughout the night of 14 March 1863. (Review of Reviews Company)

through which he could send Union vessels south around Vicksburg. Once the waterway was completed, Grant thought he would simply march his army down the river and the vessels could then ferry troops across to the eastern bank. But after several long weeks of arduous labor, he abandoned the operation. Then he put his army to work digging an alternative channel bypassing the city, through which they could redirect the river waters and float vessels south. Again, the operation failed. Next, he ordered an expedition to cut a waterway through Yazoo Pass via a bayou. When that failed, Grant put his men to work creating a waterway that ran down from Yazoo Pass at the northern end of the delta, but it was blocked by the Confederates when they constructed Fort Pemberton in its path. After weeks of monotonous laboring for nothing, one soldier called this winter 'the Valley Forge of the War.'

Although Grant's futile attempts to get at the river fortress did little to satisfy an anxious and demanding Northern public, by mid-April the commander had settled on a plan that would work. It would ultimately prove so successful that it would immortalize Grant as the great victor of Vicksburg. He would move his troops below the city, head to Jackson and cut the railroads, and then move west toward Vicksburg and seize the high ground in the rear of the city.

This picture of Benjamin H. Grierson and his men was taken shortly after his famous raid. Sitting with chin in hand, Grierson boasted of the most significant Union cavalry raid of the war in the west, luring John Pemberton's cavalry into futile pursuit. (Review of Reviews Company)

As Grant moved his forces from Milliken's Bend to below Vicksburg, Admiral David Dixon Porter, the naval commander accompanying the land expedition, sent his fleet of 12 vessels past the city on the night of 16 April. In dramatic fashion, all but one vessel managed to run past Confederate batteries and grouped together near Hard Times on the west bank of the Mississippi, where Grant's troops were concentrated. Five nights later, six Federal transports and 12 barges loaded with supplies attempted to run past the city. Although Confederate batteries sunk one transport and six barges, the operation was a success. Grant could now get his men across the river to the eastern shore.

Fifty miles (80km) south of Vicksburg, Bruinsburg, Mississippi, provided Grant with the ideal place to ferry his army across the river. Although the Confederates frustrated the initial crossing, on 30 April Grant had his army back in Mississippi poised to strike. To divert attention from his main force and to destroy Confederate supplies, Grant would need some help. Rosecrans kept Bragg sufficiently busy in Tennessee, so he could not send reinforcements to Pemberton's aid. 'Old Rosy' accomplished this by setting out on what became the Tullahoma campaign. Sherman was ordered to demonstrate against the high bluffs north of Vicksburg and would then catch up to the main force. Grant also ordered raids against the Confederates' logistics bases. One of the most successful raids was undertaken by Colonel Benjamin H. Grierson, a professional bandmaster before the war. Beginning on 17 April, Grierson's 1,700 cavalrymen started from La Grange, Mississippi, and in a few short weeks wreaked havoc all the way south to Baton Rouge, Louisiana.

Jackson, the state capital of Mississippi, was more important to Grant because four railroads intersected the city, the most important of which went to Vicksburg. Jackson provided the lifeline to the river fortress and to destroy it meant that Vicksburg would wither on the vine. Still, Pemberton commanded 52,000 soldiers and if Grant attempted to supply his 41,000-man army from Bruinsburg 40 miles (64km) away, the Confederates could easily put up a stern defense while possibly cutting the Union

Soldiers and residents alike dug into the hillsides around Vicksburg during the siege on the city. The bombproof shelters in this picture were carved out by the soldiers of the 45th Illinois. (Hulton Getty)

supply. Grant concluded then to live off the land. After all, his army had done this before in Mississippi during the winter. Now, with the growing season about to provide Southern farms with bountiful crops, there would be plenty for his troops to feed on. In addition to forage for the animals, Mississippi farms yielded corn, hogs, cattle, sheep, and poultry. Many planters had reduced the cultivation of cotton in favor of food staples.

By the second week of May, Grant's army had started east for Jackson. Resupplied and eager to move, his three corps commanded by Sherman, Major-General James B. McPherson, and himself moved along the Black River, a natural boundary that flowed north–south and east of Vicksburg and that

favored his advance. On 12 May, the Federals met resistance at Raymond, 15 miles (24km) south of Jackson. After several hours of fighting, the Confederates pulled back to the capital. The following day, Confederate General Joseph E. Johnston, recently sent to take command of all the troops in besieged Mississippi, pulled together 12,000 troops to protect Jackson. On 14 May, in a severe rainstorm, Sherman's and McPherson's corps drove the Confederates through the city and captured it by mid-afternoon. Outnumbered nearly five to one, Johnston headed north.

While Sherman's corps destroyed the city of Jackson, burning manufacturing installations, Grant ordered McPherson's corps to head west toward Vicksburg and threaten the enemy's communications. Pemberton responded to an order to join Johnston and strike a counteroffensive against Grant's army while it remained at Jackson. The Confederate commander moved a portion of his army out of Vicksburg and placed it on the railroad east of the Black River. The two Confederate forces were only miles apart.

On 16 May, just before noon, a division of Grant's army attacked Pemberton's 20,000 Confederates at Champion's Hill, a commanding ridge east of the Black River, driving them back on the left. The Confederates, however, countered and a full-scale battle ensued. McPherson's men were called up to support the Union right flank, bringing the effective Union strength to 29,000 men, and late in the day, the Federals managed to take the ridge. Pemberton fell back to the Black River, and eventually all the way to Vicksburg. On 18 May, the triumphant Federals crossed the Black River and seized the bluffs around the town. Now, having taken the high ground that skirted the town, Grant dug in.

The siege of Vicksburg

While Johnston was being reinforced by troops from Tennessee and South Carolina, Grant collected his troops and, thanks to

Halleck in Washington, also received reinforcements. Pemberton, meanwhile, was contemplating a way out of Vicksburg. Realizing that attempting to evacuate the city would not only be futile, but also give the Federals complete control of the Mississippi, Pemberton chose to stay and try to outlast the siege. Anxious to capitalize on his string of successful operations and capture the entire force and the town, Grant launched a series of quick assaults on 19 May. Within minutes the Confederates shattered the Union wave, causing about 1,000 casualties. Three days later, a determined Grant made another attempt on the town using his entire 45,000-man force, but it produced the same bloody result. Grant resolved not to assault the town again, and instead began the siege in earnest, using not only land forces but also his gunboats. 'The enemy are undoubtedly in our grasp,' wrote Grant on 24 May. 'The fall of Vicksburg and the capture of most of the garrison can only be a question of time.'

Elsewhere, Federals were on the move and shoring up their strongholds. On 21 May, Major-General Nathaniel Banks moved from Baton Rouge toward Port Hudson, below Vicksburg on the Mississippi River. His 13,000 Federals besieged the 4,500-man garrison under the command of Major-General Franklin Gardner. On 14 June, Banks ordered the garrison to surrender, and when they refused he stormed the fort, but the Confederates held strong. The siege continued. Meanwhile, on 23 June, Rosecrans moved south from Murfreesboro against Bragg's Confederates at Tullahoma. By outflanking Bragg, the Federal commander had forced him to retreat across the Tennessee River by the end of the month.

As the siege progressed, Grant attempted to break through the Confederate defenses by mining under them and blowing them up. On 25 June, Federal engineers detonated 2,200lbs of powder in a tunnel that had been run under the Third Louisiana Redan. Two Union regiments stormed into the gap, but Confederates had ordered a second defensive line slightly to the rear in case the Federals broke through, and they repelled the advancing Yankees.

By late June, Grant's communications along the Mississippi, safeguarded by gunboats, were secure and the Federal command simply waited for the Confederates to capitulate out of starvation. Day after day, artillery shells poured down on the trembling town. Trapped against the river and forced to abandon the town for the immediate countryside, the residents flocked to the nearby caves in the hills. Federals and Confederates alike wondered how long the siege would continue. Hundreds of wounded Southern soldiers were forced to remain in the Vicksburg hospitals, many of which were makeshift operations and converted abandoned homes. As the shelling continued, so too did the starvation of soldiers and citizens, many forced to eat mule meat, rats, and dogs. Most serious was the lack of fresh drinking water.

Finally, after 47 days the siege came to an end. Pemberton decided he must surrender on 4 July 1863. Grant and Pemberton had served in the same division during part of the Mexican War and the two men greeted one another as old acquaintances. When Pemberton asked for terms, Grant responded that 'the useless effusion of blood you propose stopping by this course can be ended at any time you may choose, by the unconditional surrender of the city and the garrison.' As the fatigued and disheartened Southern soldiers marched out of the city, the Federals quietly lowered the Confederate flag and raised the Stars and Stripes in its place. River vessels blew their whistles and the Union bands struck up the 'Battle Cry of Freedom.' From a distance residents watched with tears in their eyes as the jubilant Yankees went wild. Grant recalled years after the war that the capture of Vicksburg 'gave new spirit to the loyal people of the North.' Embittered Vicksburg residents did not celebrate the 4th of July again until the Second World War inspired a renewed patriotic enthusiasm and devotion for the United States.

The siege cost the Federals nearly 5,000 casualties, while the Confederates suffered significantly fewer casualties resulting from combat. The cumulative effect of the capitulation, however, handed over 29,000 soldiers to the Federal army. More important was the loss of the Confederacy's final fortress itself and the heavy equipment and small arms.

The capitulation was hailed all over the North with exuberance, especially when just a few days later Port Hudson succumbed to siege and surrendered. Capturing Port Hudson, however, had cost nearly 10,000 Union soldiers, while the Confederates had lost 871 men. The Union had reclaimed the river. 'The Father of Waters again goes unvexed to the sea,' remarked Lincoln. Not only had Lincoln been given the 'Gibraltar of the West,' but also he had found in Grant a general unlike any he had in the Eastern Theater. 'He doesn't worry and bother me,' remarked Lincoln. 'He isn't shrieking for reinforcements all the time. He takes what troops we can safely give him … and does the best he can with what he has got. And if Grant only does this thing right down there … why, Grant is my man and I am his the rest of the war.'

The summer of 1863 was a defining period in the Civil War. The campaigns in the Western Theater went a long way in determining whether or not the Confederacy would win its independence. The Union victories in the West had shaped the contours of the conflict. Much fighting had been done, but the conflict was hardly nearing an end. Equally important to the Union overall scheme in the West, Chattanooga remained in Confederate hands. Since the opening of the conflict, possession of the strategic railroad nexus and river city had been the desire of Lincoln. Positioned in the heart of East Tennessee, Chattanooga in Union hands would open the way for Union armies in the West to penetrate further into the Southern heartland. Although the Union armies were positioned to further dominate the Western Theater, it was still too soon to tell whether or not those who had fallen in the battles in the previous two and a half years had died in vain for their cause.

The capture of Vicksburg and Port Hudson cut the Confederacy in half and opened the entire Mississippi River to Union gunboats and transports. Lincoln remarked at the time that the 'Father of Waters goes unvexed to the sea.' (Hulton Getty)

Billy Yank and Johnny Reb at war

Although the United States was not prepared for the conflict that erupted in 1861, by the war's end it looked like a nation that had prepared for decades. By 1865, 3 million citizens, North and South, had mustered into military service. Volunteers from vastly diverse backgrounds flocked to enlist. Although the war was America's first modern war, it still had an agrarian character, as farmers comprised the largest numbers of volunteers on both sides. Soldiers were typically between the ages of 18 and 24, white, single, and Protestant. Although both sides employed blacks behind the lines as laborers until mid-1863, by 1865 roughly 180,000 blacks had fought in the Union army. Immigrants, mostly Germans and Irish, also participated in the conflict. Western states contributed large numbers of immigrants to the cause.

The Civil War was a conflict fought mainly between foot soldiers. Nearly 80 percent of Union fighting men were infantrymen, with 14 percent serving as cavalry and the remaining 6 percent serving in the artillery. Seventy-five percent of the soldiers in the

Confederacy were infantrymen, 20 per cent served in the cavalry, and 5 per cent served with artillery units.

One of the reasons that the war was so fiercely contested was because soldiers of both armies came to believe they were fighting for a common cause: personal liberties, constitutional guarantees, democratic principles, and republican ideals. Still, some 630,000 soldiers lost their lives over conflicting means of achieving the same ends.

Pride in country and state induced men to volunteer, and Union soldiers often

In a typical regimental portrait, these soldiers of the 125th Ohio Volunteers reflect the worn yet determined character of the men who fought the war between the Appalachian Mountains and the Mississippi River. (Massachusetts Commandery Military Order of the Loyal Legion and the US Army Military History Institute)

expressed their devotion to the cause by using patriotic rhetoric. 'The cause for which the majority of men now in the army have enlisted to defend is sacred,' wrote an Illinoisan. 'I consider that we should do what we can for the cause for which we enlisted and strive on until it is accomplished.' A Louisianian concluded, 'I had rather fall in this cause than to see my country dismantled of its glory and independence – for of its honor it cannot be deprived.'

Political, social, and economic reasons also inspired men to join the military. Many men volunteered because they believed it was the virtuous thing to do to protect their local communities, their homes, families, and friends. The army also offered perhaps a more satisfying and financially rewarding life than the boredom and fatigue of struggling to till the soil. Because the nation was in the midst of a depression when the war began, army pay was quite attractive. A Union private received $13 a month and a Confederate private received $11 a month, and both governments provided incentives in the way of bounties or bonuses to enlist for longer periods. Because many enlistees were unmarried, the adventure of traversing the countryside and the chance of potentially becoming a hero was an additional motivation. Politics also motivated men to fight and often found expression in anti-slavery sentiments. 'Old John Brown Set this war in motion, and threw himself beneath ... as the first martyr,' declared Orrin Stebbins, 'and it will never Stop until that dark Stane of African Slavery is wiped out so dry.'

Army life

Because Civil War soldiers were extensions of their local communities, they adopted symbols, uniforms, names, and flags reflective of these prewar associations that gave a unit an identity. Several Northern units adopted the Zouave uniform worn by French troops. It consisted of a red turban

Lew Wallace, famous after the Civil War as the author of *Ben Hur*, commented about the Zouave uniforms of the 11th Indiana Regiment, which bore his name as the 'Wallace Zouaves': 'There was nothing of the flashy Algerian colors in the uniform of the Eleventh Indiana; no red fez, no red breeches, no red or yellow sash with tassels big as early cabbages. Our outfit was of the tamest grey twilled goods, not unlike home made jeans – a visor cap, French in pattern, its top of red cloth not larger than the palm of one's hand; a blue flannel shirt with open neck, a jacket Greekish in form. edged with narrow binding, the red scarcely noticeable; breeches baggy but not petticoated; button gaiters connecting below the knees with the breeches, and strapped over the shoes.'(Painting by Don Troiani, www.historicalartprints.com)

with white band and orange tinsel, a short blue jacket with gold trimming, loose red trousers and yellow buckskin leggings. The 11th Indiana Zouaves, known as the 'Wallace Zouaves' in honor of their commander, Lew Wallace, wore a midwestern variation of the uniform. Still, whatever their specific unit identities, Northerners became known as 'Billy Yanks,' and Southerners became known as 'Johnny Rebs.'

In the tradition of their democratic heritage, soldiers were allowed to elect many of their officers, while some were appointed by politicians. Of course, this presented problems as friends or enemies-turned-soldiers could find taking orders from these persons awkward. The core of military life, however, was discipline and uniformity, both of which caused problems for the typical soldier. Disrespect for authority was the first and most common offense committed by men of blue and gray. Although both governments attempted to nationalize their armies, Northerners proved more amenable to adherence to regulations and nationalism than did Southerners.

Varied uniforms and equipment became a problem, and soon the governments enforced a standardized code in both. Because gray had been the popular color of militia and cadet uniforms in the prewar years, both sides initially marched off in variations of the same color. The Union would eventually adopt blue as the official uniform color, as that had been the color of uniforms in the professional army. Confederates would eventually adopt gray as their national color.

Because most soldiers marched through landscapes that were vastly different from their local communities, soldiers were initially awed by the grandeur of their surroundings. Camps were where soldiers spent the bulk of their time, and they became both homes and training grounds, filled with excitement at some times and endless monotony at others. The discipline of drill and training could prove the difference between life and death in combat, so soldiers spent hours each day drilling and preparing for the inevitable fight. Soldiers in the Western Theater typically slept in tents or huts, depending on the weather. The shelter tent or 'dog tent,' as it was commonly known for its small size, was the standard issue by 1862. Soldiers rose at 5.00 am, assembled, drilled, ate breakfast, then went to their assigned duties. The bugle sounded lunch at noon, and regimental drill followed for two to three hours. Soldiers then returned to their quarters until dress parade at 6.00 pm, followed by dinner and free time until 9.00 pm.

Soldiers spent their free time writing letters home, detailing their reactions to their new surroundings, politics, and emotions about missing home. When they were not writing, they were reading dime novels and newspapers from home or national newspapers, including the popular pictorial papers such as *Frank Leslie's Illustrated*, *Harper's Weekly*, and *Southern Illustrated News*. Soldiers frequently indulged in playing cards, horse racing, drinking, fist-fighting, story-telling, animal chasing, and other irreverent activities to escape the loneliness of army life.

When time permitted, theatrical productions gave the men immense pleasure. *Bombasties Furioso*, a farce staged by the Confederate 9th Kentucky, was the hit of the 1862–63 season in the west.

Singing was as popular as letter writing, and soldiers were just as expressive in song as they were in writing. Soldiers voiced their longing for home, their patriotism to the cause, and their sentimental feeling for the fight. Billy Yank and Johnny Reb alike sang 'Home, Sweet Home,' 'The Girl I Left Behind,' and 'When This Cruel War is Over.' 'The Bonnie Blue Flag' and 'Dixie' were popular with Confederates and Federals enjoyed 'Yankee Doodle' and 'The Battle Hymn of the Republic.' Northern soldiers passed the hours marching to the popular tune 'John Brown's Body.' At the beginning of the war, brass

Brass bands accompanied many units into the Civil War and soldiers came to greatly appreciate them. Here the 'Tiger Band' of the 125th Ohio Regiment poses for a picture. (Massachusetts Commandery Military Order of the Loyal Legion and the US Army Military History Institute)

bands accompanied many units into service, and they were constant sources of entertainment throughout the conflict.

The novelty of camp life soon wore off, however, and during the long indistinguishable days of boring life, preachers and camp chaplains attempted to maintain morale among the ranks. Religion proved to be the link between the home front and the battlefront. When all else failed, faith in God provided hope that life might improve. Army chaplains on both sides received officer status and substantial pay – $100 per month in the Union and $80 in the Confederacy. Still, they were forced to live a spartan life and, as the war continued, both sides suffered chronic shortages of qualified chaplains. Nonetheless, whether they attended Sunday service or not, Civil War soldiers relied on scriptures and faith to get them through combat. Pennsylvanian Milton Ray expressed a typical sentiment to his sister: 'I hope you may continue in earnest prayer for the preservation of my life if it is God's holy will that I should be spared ... Pray that I may be a faithful soldier of the cross and of my country.'

Death and disease

If the daily routine of harsh drilling and unrelenting discipline, the indistinguishable days of boredom, and the lack of good-quality, plentiful food that made up a soldier's camp life did not kill him, then disease or disability from a battle-inflicted wound often did. Of the 360,222 Union men who died in the war, over 250,000 deaths resulted from disease; nearly three-quarters of the Confederate casualties also perished to disease. Because camp sites were chosen for military and not health considerations, soldiers suffered tremendous depredations. Inadequate drainage, ignorance of sanitary practices, and the natural carelessness associated with army life characterized Union and Confederate camps and produced a contaminated atmosphere. 'We have had an awful time drinking the meanest water not fit for a horse (indeed I could hardly get my horse to drink it),' remarked a Texas surgeon.

Measles, smallpox, typhoid, diarrhea, malaria, and dysentery were prevalent throughout the war. More than 1,700,000 cases of diarrhea were recorded by Federal doctors during the war, and 57,000 proved fatal. Because many soldiers were farm boys who had largely escaped a host of communicable diseases, these spread like epidemics in camp. Soldiers, uneducated about the importance of hygiene, exacerbated their problems by not bathing or changing their clothes. Army surgeons were few in number and their limited knowledge and medical supplies often combined to make the attempt to save a life as fatal as the attempt to take one. Amputations were common.

In early May 1862, Corinth highlighted the familiar consequences of war. After the bloody two-day battle at Shiloh, the Confederates attempted to recover from the devastating effects of the battle. Corinth, a small railroad junction in northern Mississippi, was in no way prepared to accommodate 20,000 sick and wounded Confederate soldiers. Residents used every building possible to accommodate the wounded men. However, more soldiers died during the seven-week stay at Corinth than had fallen in two days of battle. A Confederate nurse, Kate Cumming, was at the Tishomingo Hotel in Corinth, where she found scores of disabled soldiers, 'mutilated in every imaginable way.' She recalled that the wounded soldiers were lying on the bloody floors so close together that it was difficult to avoid stepping on them.

During the siege of Vicksburg in May–July 1863, countless Confederate soldiers and civilians fell victim to disease. Despite herculean attempts to administer to the wounded, the city and military hospitals, with cots arranged even outside on the grounds, could not take care of the flow of casualties from the trenches. Scarcely a woman at Vicksburg was not involved in ministering to the wounded.

More pathetic than the soldiers in hospitals suffering from disease were the soldiers who suffered on the battlefield. Before the fight soldiers wrestled with fear, often pinning their name and unit on their shirts. Even the most seasoned veteran was routinely shocked by the grisly aftermath. The Battle of Shiloh baptized the soldiers and the country in the vast number of ways men could be killed. Before the battle, one Tennessean penned in his diary, 'I shall never forget how I felt that day ... knowing that with the early tomorrow many of us most likely would pass away.' In many respects, experiencing combat cured the anxious soldier's desire to 'see the elephant,' as fighting in battle was commonly known. The end of a battle often brought exhaustion and the realization that the soldier's unit had suffered tremendous losses.

Because regimental surgeons had to perform frequent amputations of arms and legs, a kit specifically designed for amputations such as the one in this picture was standard issue for military doctors. (Painting by Don Troiani, www.historicalartprints.com)

The common soldiers who fought the war were the unsung heroes of camp and combat. Americans who were otherwise ordinary became heroes in many ways, simply because they endured the ordeal and penned something of their experience. The war became central to their peacetime lives and to the lives of their children and grandchildren. 'What an experience the last few years have been!' wrote a Wisconsin soldier. 'I would not take any amount of money & have the events which have transpired in that length of time blotted out from my memory.'

John Beatty, a Union soldier

In many ways, John Beatty typified the common soldier of the Union army, and his journal details army life in the Western Theater throughout the early years of the war. Beatty was born on 16 December 1828 near Sandusky in the western region of Ohio, a region known for its strong anti-slavery sentiments. At the outbreak of war, he raised a company of local volunteers, which joined the 3rd Ohio Volunteer Infantry Regiment.

When the unit was mustered into service, Beatty, recently promoted to lieutenant-colonel, became the regiment's commander. In November 1861, however, his regiment was transferred to General Don Carlos Buell's Army of the Ohio in Kentucky. Throughout 1862 and 1863, he campaigned across the Bluegrass state, Tennessee, northern Mississippi, and northern Alabama, participating in many of the battles. At

33 years of age, Beatty was older than the typical soldier who mustered into the army in 1861, and at 5 feet 11 inches, he was taller than most mid-nineteenth-century Americans. He was thin, possessed dark hair, and wore a mustache, characteristic of Civil War soldiers.

Like most soldiers, Beatty typically began his journal entries with comments about the climate. 'The weather has been delightful, warm as spring time. The nights are beautiful' is representative of the remarks he frequently made. The landscape was also a source of interest. 'This is peculiar country,' he remarked while in Louisville, 'there are innumerable caverns, and every few rods places are found where the crust of the earth appears to have broken and sunk down hundreds of feet.'

Beatty was also struck by the obvious and routine role that slavery played in the lives of the Southern people. Upon arriving in Louisville, Beatty came across a sign that read 'Negroes Bought and Sold,' and this struck a cord with the Ohioan. 'We have known to be sure, that negroes were bought and sold, like cattle and tobacco, but it nevertheless, awakened new, and not by any means agreeable, sensations to see the humiliating fact announced on the broad side of a commercial house.' To this he added, 'These signs must come down.'

Beatty found camp life both rewarding and a nuisance. It was rewarding to enjoy the weather of the South and to hear the pleasantries of music under moonlit nights. 'The boys are in a happier mood, and a round, full voice comes to us from the tents with the words of an old Scotch song.' Still, it was difficult to keep the men out of trouble. 'The boys, out of pure devilment, set fire to the leaves, and to-night the forest was illuminated.' In August 1862, he wrote: 'I am weak, discouraged, and worn out with idleness.' Excessive drinking often brought retribution and insubordination from the soldiers. When Beatty arrested a half-drunk soldier and strapped him to a tree for being insolent, the soldiers reacted scornfully. 'It was a high-handed outrage upon the person of a volunteer soldier,' Beatty observed, and the common soldiers never let their commanders forget they were volunteers.

There were also casualties beyond the battlefield for the soldiers of Beatty's regiment. When a soldier got a letter from home that his girlfriend had married someone else, Beatty remarked that the news made this soldier 'crazy as a loon.' The poor

When Confederate General Braxton Bragg marched into Kentucky in the summer of 1862, Union General Don Carlos Buell was forced to pursue him and to build bridges across the rivers. In this picture, Buell's troops are crossing the Big Barren River. Here the 19th Michigan Engineers had to reconstruct the bridge by using pontoons located in the middle of the river. (Review of Reviews Company)

soul 'imagined that he was in hell, thought Dr Seyes the devil, and so violent did he become that they had to bind him.' Worse yet was the disease of the soldiers, particularly during the winter months. 'There is a great deal of sickness among the troops; many cases of colds, rheumatism, and fever, resulting from exposure,' Beatty observed. 'Passing through the company quarters of our regiment at midnight, I was alarmed by the constant and heavy coughing of the men. I fear the winter will send many more to the grave than the bullets of the enemy, for a year to come.' It surely did.

Beatty also noted that the Union army had become a haven for runaway slaves. 'We have much trouble with the escaped negroes … the colored folks get into our regimental lines, and in some mysterious way are so disposed of that their masters never hear of them again.' Near Murfreesboro, Tennessee, he remarked: 'We have in our camp a superabundance of negroes.'

During spells of boredom, Beatty usually turned his thoughts 'to the cottage home, to wife and children, to a time still further away when we had no children, when we were making the preliminary arrangements for starting the world together, when her cheeks were ruddier than now, when wealth and fame and happiness seemed lying just before me, ready to be gathered in, and farther away still, to a gentle, blue-eyed mother – now long gone – teaching her child to lisp his first prayer.' Religion often found expression in music and was a way for the men to escape the boredom of camp life. 'Surely nothing has the power to make us forget earth and its round of troubles as these sweet old church songs, familiar from earliest childhood,' commented Beatty.

Beatty read the newspapers and was particularly interested in the politics of the war. In July 1862, the Ohioan commented on the Confiscation Act passed by the Congress. 'I trust the new policy indicated by the confiscation act, just passed by Congress, will have a good effect.' 'It will, at least, enable us to weaken the enemy,' he argued, 'and strengthen ourselves, as we have

hitherto not been able to do.' 'Slavery is the enemy's weak point, the key to his position. If we can tear down this institution, the rebels will lose all interest in the Confederacy, and be too glad to escape with their lives …'

He clearly viewed the institution of slavery as the cause of the war and the root of the evils of Southern society. By the end of 1862, the Emancipation Proclamation had clearly changed the war. In February 1863, Beatty remarked that the 'army is turning its attention to politics somewhat,' particularly when it came to Lincoln's Proclamation. 'Generals and colonels are ventilating their opinions through the press. I think their letters may have a good effect upon the people at home, and prevent them from discouraging the army and crippling the Administration.'

Beatty also wrote about commanders. For the most part he liked his division commander, General Ormsby Mitchel. Mitchel was a professional and proper gentleman who 'never drinks and never swears,' and in Beatty's estimation was 'indefatigable.' But Beatty came to detest Don Carlos Buell for his slowness in campaigning and for his apparent sympathy with the Southern people during the summer of 1862. Buell 'is inaugurating the dancing-master policy,' which was Beatty's sarcastic expression for Buell's lethargy, which he declared was the policy of an 'idiot.'

Campaigning gave Beatty plenty of things to react to, not the least of which was the unexpected cheering of citizens for the Union soldiers. 'We passed many fine houses, and extensive, well improved farms,' he penned in 1862, 'but few white people were seen. The negroes appeared to have entire possession.' The sight of a pretty woman warmed his heart. While marching in Tennessee, Beatty came upon a scene where 'a young and very pretty girl stood in the doorway of a handsome farm-house and waved the Union flag. Cheer after cheer arose along the line; officers saluted, soldiers waved their hats, and the bands played "Yankee Doodle" and "Dixie." ' 'That loyal girl,' he wrote, 'captured a thousand hearts.' Seeing his first cotton field was given space in his dairy.

Murfreesboro, Tennessee, was quite a place for Beatty. He remarked:

Murfreesboro is an aristocratic town, many of the citizens have as fine carriages as are to be seen in Cincinnati or Washington. On pleasant week-day evenings they sometimes come out to witness the parades. The ladies, so far as I can judge by a glimpse through a carriage window, are richly and elegantly dressed. The poor whites are as poor as rot, and the rich are very rich. There is no substantial well-to-do middle class. The slaves are, in fact, the middle class here.

By April 1863, however, Murfreesboro had undergone a transformation. The fine houses and trees of the city had been 'cut or trampled down and destroyed.' 'Many frame houses, and very good ones, too,' he remarked, 'have been torn down, and the lumber and timber used in the construction of hospitals.' Even the air had changed: 'There is a fearful stench in many places near here, arising from decaying horses and mules.'

Perhaps nothing caught Beatty's attention more than the ordeal of the battle. In February 1862, he wrote that although it was bitterly cold, 'the conviction that a battle was imminent kept the men steady and prevented straggling.' The evening before the Battle of Stone's River (Murfreesboro) in December 1862, Beatty wrote: 'To-morrow, doubtless, the grand battle will be fought, when I trust the good Lord will grant us a glorious victory, and one that will make glad hearts of all loyal people on New-Year's Day.' At one point during the battle, he glanced up to see a soldier who was heading to the back of the line struck in the back between the shoulders, killing him instantly.

After the battle he walked the battlefield and found the dead and wounded scattered for miles. As he walked across the terrain, he commented: 'we find men with their legs shot off; one with his brains scooped out with a cannon ball; another with half a face

The Rutherford County courthouse in Murfreesboro, Tennessee. The courthouse reflects the aristocratic facade of the Tennessee town that so impressed soldiers like Ohio's John Beatty. The Battle of Stone's River was fought near the courthouse, which was converted into a hospital for Braxton Bragg's forces. (Review of Reviews Company)

gone; another with entrails protruding ... another boy lies with his hands clasped above his head, indicating that his last words were a prayer.' 'How many poor men moaned through the cold nights in the thick woods, where the first day's battle occurred,' he penned, 'calling in vain to man for help, and finally making their last solemn petition to God!'

The fact that Beatty survived the Civil War was a testament to his fitness as an officer and to a significant degree the result of simple luck. When he resigned his commission in January 1864 and returned to Sandusky, the Civil War became central to his life. An everyday banker from Ohio who had witnessed the drama of the Civil War, Beatty was no longer an ordinary citizen.

Societies at war

The sectional conflict was an extraordinary military undertaking and the composition and conduct of Civil War armies revealed much about the communities from which they came. The 3 million men who participated in the war came to appreciate the struggles of their local communities to sustain the war effort and their daily lives. While fierce battles ravaged the landscape, Americans North and South fought a war behind the lines that produced its own heroes, who distinguished themselves by performing the labor necessary to maintain the war effort. Shortly after the Battle of Stone's River, New Yorker George Templeton Strong summed up perhaps the Union's most distinguishing advantage in the war. 'It may have been indecisive,' he remarked in referring to the battle, 'but our resources will stand the wear and tear of indecisive conflict longer than those of slavedom, and can sooner be repaired.'

Economic and military resources

For a nation that was not prepared to wage war, in a short time Northerners and Southerners made effective use of the economic and technological advances afforded them by the industrial revolution. They forged these economic weapons with a fighting determination that produced what has often been considered the first modern war. Economic and technological influences directly shaped the conduct of the war, and political leaders came to appreciate the role that the government could play in harnessing these influences. As the industrial revolution generated massive quantities of goods, American manufacturers benefited from the purchase of arms and the wide

array of other supplies needed to wage war on an enormous scale.

Such changes also left an indelible mark on the home front. 'On every street and avenue,' commented a *Chicago Tribune* reporter, 'one sees new buildings going up, immense stone, brick, and iron business blocks, marble palaces and new residences everywhere manifest … where the enterprise of man can gain a foothold.' Shoes fitted for each foot, canned foods, and sewing machines all reflected the arrival of new technologies. Pennsylvania's iron industry increased its output of rails by 50 percent during the war, and Pittsburgh

became the nation's leading iron producer. This increased production made possible the raising, supplying, and resupplying of the large number of troops in the field. In a war that was fought mainly by farmers on both sides, agricultural production actually increased between 1861 and 1865. This increase was due in part to an increase in agricultural machinery, which assisted Northern farmers in producing bumper crops throughout the war.

Throughout the course of the war, the quartermaster struggled to supply 2.3 million Union soldiers and 1 million Confederates who daily desired armaments and basic necessities such as bread, meat, shoes, and clothes. Factory production, North and South, expanded to meet these military demands. Although railroads could be used to transport goods to supply bases, in many cases armies relied on riverboats and animal-drawn wagons to transport supplies. This presented numerous logistical problems because the further the army marched away from its supply base, the more vulnerable it became to enemy sabotage. In the summer of 1862, Don Carlos Buell required nearly 15 miles (24km) of supply wagons to keep his Army of the Ohio equipped and fed.

What armies lacked in transporting efficiency, they more than compensated for by effectively utilizing the telegraph during the Civil War to assist in coordinating such transport burdens. This communicative device was another new technological feature of the industrial revolution. From

Thanks to the telegraph, armies were able to set up communications anywhere in the field. The poles they used varied in height, but were placed 5ft (1.5m) into the ground to resist high winds. (Ann Ronan Picture Library)

1861 to 1865 the United States Military Telegraph constructed some 15,000 miles (24,000km) of military lines. Due to a lack of operators and wire, Confederates managed to construct only about 500 miles (800km) in lines. In some cases, telegraph officers in the South were employed by companies in the North. Telegraphic communications were particularly vital to the scattered armies in the Western Theater. From St Louis, Missouri, Henry Halleck was able to communicate with Buell in Kentucky and Grant in Tennessee, and ordered them to concentrate their armies during the spring of 1862.

More than any other advance in early modern warfare, the rifled firearms of the Civil War proved the most destructive. The devastation inflicted by this new firepower reduced artillery to the defense, rendered the open frontal assault suicidal, and made entrenching a battlefield a necessity. Although both sides embraced this tactical consideration, some generals still ordered frontal assaults throughout the war. Braxton Bragg ordered a dozen such assaults at the Battle of Shiloh against the Hornet's Nest. The result was mass slaughter. By the war's end, it could be said that the rifled musket had caused some 60 Union regiments, and a higher number of Confederate ones, the loss of more than 50 percent of their men in a single engagement.

The role of women

Another noticeable sign that the war had wrought social change was evidenced by the new roles for women. Not only did Northern and Southern women enter factories, sewing rooms, and arsenals, but also they tended farms and plantations, and became saloon keepers, steamboat captains, bankers, teamsters, teachers, and morticians. Women also entered the war zone as nurses, clerks, and copyists, and some even disguised themselves as men and mustered into the ranks as soldiers. By 1864, Union women held down one-third of all the jobs in the manufacturing workplace. Still, they received

lower wages than the men who had previously held those jobs. Although most of their employment gains did not endure after the war, as demobilized troops returned to the workforce, the wartime experience of women broke them forever out of the traditional domestic sphere.

Women were also employed as spies. A shrewd actress, Pauline Cushman, used her art well to play the part of a spy. Although a native of New Orleans, she had spent considerable time in the North and was devoted to the Union cause. Because of her knowledge of the terrain and roads of Tennessee, Mississippi, and Alabama, the Federal government gave her employment. In the summer and fall of 1861, she hunted for Southern sympathizers and spies in Louisville, and she would perform the same service in Nashville. In May 1863, as William Rosecrans was preparing to drive Braxton Bragg out of Tennessee, Cushman was captured and sentenced to hang, but managed to escape. For her services during the war, the soldiers called her 'major,' and granted her the accoutrements of the rank.

Finances

Both Union and Confederate governments pursued the same avenues to raise money to support the war, including loans, war bonds, taxes, and paper money. In the fall and winter of 1861–62, the Union coordinated its economic and financial efforts to sustain the more than 600,000 soldiers in the field. They mobilized their resources and gave an organizational structure to financing the war effort. The Republicans in power met the demand for increased production by increasing the nation's purchasing power. The Federal Congress passed the Legal Tender Act in February 1862, which authorized the issuance of $150 million in government notes ('greenbacks', as they were commonly known) that were to be used in nearly all transactions. It also increased income tax, imposed a series of excise taxes, and raised tariffs. President Lincoln relied on

A native of New Orleans, Pauline Cushman's knowledge of the roads in Tennessee, Alabama, Mississippi, and Georgia and her prewar acting experience made her an asset to the Union cause as a spy. For her contributions, the soldiers referred to her as 'major.' (Review of Reviews Company)

prominent Philadelphian Jay Cooke to market war bonds. In 1863, the government passed the National Banking Act, attempting to create a uniform national currency, and additional legislation followed in 1864 that eliminated state banknotes from circulation. The Union continued to provide for its citizens on the home front by making western lands available to free white settlers in the Homestead Act, and in the Pacific Railroad Act provided governmental support for the construction of the transcontinental railroad that had brought about bleeding Kansas in the mid-1850s.

As the size and substance of the Federal government increased, however, so the gap between the poor, the middle class, and the rich widened. Clever and innovative captains of industry, corporations, and business accumulated enormous fortunes from the war effort. Although the truly spectacular profits went to relatively few entrepreneurs, the flourishing businesses, high dividends, and massive employment spread extraordinary prosperity throughout much of the Northern population. The *New York Times* remarked that, even while a war of herculean proportions was being waged, 'the people of the North had never enjoyed a better life.'

Such economic prosperity, however, did not always equate with honest intentions. The Union government, with its newfound prosperity, was more than ever vulnerable to corruption. Colonel Andrew Jackson Butler (brother of General Benjamin F. Butler, commander of occupied New Orleans in 1862) was believed to be one of the most shameless cotton agents in the North and South. Social critics noticed the war's ability to tear at the moral fabric of society. Gambling, drinking, and prostitution were among the most prominent acts of a relaxed atmosphere. A correspondent to *The Times* of London commented that the war 'has brought the levity of the American character out in bold relief ... The indulgence in every variety of pleasure, luxury, and extravagance is simply shocking.'

The nature of the Southern economy and political alignments were not conducive to such nationalistic efforts, and the fact that the war was being waged in the South suppressed the visual displays of gratification that characterized Northern cities. Within the first year of the war, devastated factories, railroads, towns, and occupied cities such as Nashville and New Orleans, together with a naval blockade, made Southern residents feel the severity of war. Not only did the Confederacy lack the financial resources and institutions to generate a financial plan, but also the states resisted giving the central government an increased power of the purse. Confederate leaders turned to war bonds and printing paper money to compensate for their financial deficiencies.

In 1861 and 1862, the Confederate Congress approved the printing of over half a billion dollars, which accounted for more than 60 percent of the income of the Confederate war effort, but also brought dramatic inflation. Additionally, the Congress taxed consumer goods, personal income, and wholesale profits. Farmers could pay their taxes in agricultural products, known as a 'tax in kind.' As the war progressed and the financial resources waned, citizens held auctions, raffles, and drawings to raise money for the war effort. However, getting the supplies to the troops proved as unwieldy as collecting them from the civilian populace, and often tons of food rotted because of the obstacles in transporting it.

Southern farmers were increasingly forced to shift from cotton production to foodstuffs and livestock, which contributed to the war effort, but nonetheless impoverished many whites. In March 1863, the Confederate Congress passed the Impressment Act, which legalized the military seizure of private supplies of food crops. In response to the shortages of goods and exorbitant prices, a bread riot broke out in Richmond in April 1863. In the early phase of the war, the Southern populace participated in picnics, barbecues, and quilting parties as expressions of support for the war, but as the conflict endured, it smothered Southern life and social occasions became, as one historian argues, 'starvation parties.'

Politics

Although the Confederate nation lacked the two-party system of its Northern counterpart, the Southern populace, nonetheless, remained divided politically over issues relating to the central government's efforts to wage war. No issue polarized the Southern populace more than the Conscription Act of 1862. Georgia Governor Joseph E. Brown spoke for many citizens in condemning the Act. 'The late act of Congress, if executed in this State,' he

FRANK LESLIE'S ILLUSTRATED NEWSPAPER.

One of the most famous and most widely read pictorial newspapers of the war
was *Frank Leslie's Illustrated Newspaper*. (Library of Congress)

fumed to President Davis, 'does gross
injustice to a large class of her citizens,
utterly destroys all State military
organizations, and encroaches upon the
reserved rights of the State.'

The press never let Americans forget that
the war was simply politics by other means.
The correspondents who followed the armies
in the west, collectively known in the Union
as the 'Bohemian Brigade,' a characterization
of their freewheeling lifestyles, kept
Americans abreast of daily happenings in the
army. At every turn, newspapers informed the
nation not only of the military implications
of winning or losing the war, but also of how
far societies were willing to go in sacrificing
personal liberties for the cause. Although
overwhelmingly pro-Confederate, the
Southern press was divided in its attitudes to
how the war was being waged. Many
editors vehemently disagreed with President
Davis's handling of the war and bitterly
criticized him. In the case of the Union,
newspapers portrayed political leaders as
people who wanted to use the armies as a
political tool.

From the very onset of the crisis, however,
like much of the Northern populace, Lincoln
was forced to remain focused on the nature
of the conflict and the conduct of his armies.
The President's own party was divided about
what kind of war the Union should wage.
Moderates hoped to preserve the Union and
keep the war limited, believing that this
would bring about a more harmonious
reunion once the conflict ended. Radicals,
whose ranks constituted many prominent
abolitionists such as the Pennsylvanian
Thaddeus Stevens, considered the war an
opportunity to refashion society as a whole
by emancipating slaves. Lincoln sought to
placate residents of the Upper South,
particularly Democrats of the region, by
keeping the war limited to a conflict of
armies. Democrats maintained their support
for the Union as long as it remained the
same Union throughout the war and neither
expanded the war nor abridged the rights of
the citizens, whether in the Confederacy or
the Union.

Emancipation

By July 1862, however, the experience of the
war and the reaction of Southerners to
campaigning armies attempting to occupy
vast Southern regions, particularly in the
west, brought about a change in Union war
aims. No longer content to respect the civil
guarantees of the Southern rebels, the
Federal Congress passed the Confiscation
Act. It was a bold step against slavery, as it
provided freedom for slaves of rebel masters,
and it marked the turning point in the
Union's attitude to emancipation as a
precondition for ending the war and moving
toward reunion. After the Battle of Antietam
in September 1862, Lincoln issued his formal
Emancipation Proclamation, giving the
South until 1 January 1863 to return to the
Union or confront emancipation. In the end,
however, the President confided that 'if I
could save the Union without freeing any
slaves, I would do it; and if I could do it by
freeing some and leaving others alone, I
would also do that. What I do about slavery
and the colored race, I do because I believe it
helps to save this Union.'

Like the pressure for emancipation,
opposition to emancipation manifested itself
in many ways throughout the remainder of
the war. The situation in the west gave the
Republicans most concern, particularly in
Illinois and Indiana, where Democratic-
controlled legislatures threatened to pull
their troops out of the war unless Lincoln
backed down on emancipation. Democrats
opposed to emancipation bemoaned
Lincoln's handling of the war and called for
a negotiated peace to end the conflict. These
'Peace Democrats,' dubbed Copperheads by
their opponents, used the Emancipation
Proclamation, conscription, Lincoln's
suspension of the writ of Habeas Corpus, and
the string of Union defeats in the east to
build formidable opposition against him.
The most celebrated Copperhead was Ohio
Congressman Clement L. Vallandigham,
who was arrested for making anti-war
comments during his campaign for the
governorship of Ohio.

President Lincoln's Emancipation Proclamation broke the shackles of the Southern slaves. 'And upon this act,' read the proclamation, 'sincerely believed to be an act of justice, warranted by the Constitution upon military necessity, I invoke the considerable judgement of mankind, and the gracious favor of Almighty God.' (Hulton Getty)

Evidence that the war had brought significant social change could also be found in the fact that blacks were mustered into the Union ranks. Still, the lives of free blacks outside of the military remained relatively unchanged by the war. Coupled with the war's devastation of Southern infrastructure, however, within a few short months Southerners felt the markedly significant impact of emancipation. Although freedom had arrived with the Union army, in many cases it proved as much a curse as a blessing. A Union commander at Vicksburg witnessed a group of emancipated slaves. 'The scenes were appalling: the refugees were crowded together, sickly, disheartened, dying on the street, not a family of them all either well sheltered, clad or fed; no physicians, no medicines, no hospitals; many of the persons who had been charged with feeding them either sick or dead.' Like slavery, freedom

had a price and according to the commander, 'the great multitude were unprepared to work beyond supplying their immediate necessities ... Their minds were not adjusted to the new situation.'

The longer the war lasted, the more striking was the evidence of loss. Southerners experienced directly the severity of the Union's aims, precisely because it was their slaves whom Lincoln emancipated. As the situation on the battlefront and the home front became more desperate, more desperate measures were enacted. Both governments enacted conscription during the war. The Confederacy was first to authorize such a draft in 1862, followed the next year by the Union. Still, the absence of white males from the Southern economy took its toll early on. In an attempt to secure his son's release from the army, an elderly Southern father wrote to the War Department that 'If you dount send him home I am bound to louse my crop and cum to suffer.' At home, residents held Congregational prayer meetings, pleading for success in the war effort.

In many cases, the Confederate soldiers appeared to many residents as the invading horde they were supposed to repel. In

January 1863, a Louisiana planter reacted with scorn when a Confederate brigade made his home their campsite. 'Our troops have stripped me, by robbery, of nearly every resource for living from day to day, & what is in reserve for me from the common enemy, is yet to be ascertained,' he remarked. 'From a condition of ease, comfort and abundance, I am suddenly reduced to one of hardship, want & privation.'

By the summer of 1863, southerners in the West had succumbed to a world the war made. Slaves experienced the dawning of a new day, while whites tried in vain to escape the endless nightmare. As the Union armies traversed the

Clement Vallandigham was the unofficial leader of the Copperheads, a name given to the Northern peace movement during the Civil War. He opposed Lincoln's election in 1860 and protested Republican war measures so vehemently that he was finally arrested in 1863. Lincoln commuted his sentence and sent him South, but he made his way to Canada, where he unsuccessfully ran for the governorship of Ohio. (Ann Ronan Picture Library)

countryside in the west, they engaged in two fights – combat and occupation – winning both. Southerners experienced monumental losses of property, slaves, and homes, but they endured. It had become clear by this time that the revolutionaries had become victims of the revolution.

Kate Stone, a Confederate civilian

Kate Stone was 20 years old when the Civil War broke out. She was living with her widowed mother, five brothers, and younger sister at Brokenburn, a 1,200-acre cotton plantation in northeast Louisiana, about 30 miles (48km) northwest of Vicksburg, Mississippi. The Stones owned 150 slaves and their antebellum plantation life imbued strong devotion to the Confederate cause in 1861. Kate began writing her diary in May 1861 and it chronicles the hardships she and her family endured until they were forced to leave Louisiana as a result of the Vicksburg campaign in the summer of 1863.

In 1861, Kate was coming of age and keenly aware of the significance of her times and of her own maturation as woman. The war threatened her family's affluence and social status, and her chances of marriage. She resented the fact that the Confederate army mobilized three out of four white males in the South, including her brother and uncle, leaving behind mostly women and slaves to conduct the affairs of economic and social life. Kate was dissatisfied with her isolation on the plantation. 'When quietly our days are passing,' she commiserated, 'when the whole planet is in such a state of feverish excitement and everywhere there is the stir and mob of angry life – O! to see and be in it all.' 'I hate weary days of inaction,' she remarked, 'yet what can women do but wait and suffer?'

Although Kate recognized that life would be difficult for the soldiers, remarking that 'They go to bear all hardships, to brave all dangers, and to face death in every form,' she soon learned that the home front could be just as challenging as the battlefront. 'We who stay behind,' she wrote, 'may find it harder than they who go. They will have new scenes and constant excitement to buoy them up and the consciousness of duty

done.' Still, the waiting and the monotony were exasperating. 'No war news or any other kind. Oh, this inactive life when there is such a stir and excitement in the busy world outside. It is enough to run one wild. Oh! to be in the heat and turmoil of it all, to live, to live, not stagnate here.'

For Kate, writing was a way to participate. But as the war closed in on her world, she came to feel the attack, the occupation, and the devastation of thousands of Southerners in the west. As early as May 1861, Kate commented that 'Times are already dreadfully hard.'

The press made an impact on Kate, particularly because she came to believe that Northern papers had terribly misrepresented the South. 'The Northern papers do make us mad!' she commented in May 1861. 'Why will they tell such horrible stories about us?' One of the most significant changes on the plantation was the change in attitude among the slaves. 'The runaways are numerous and bold.' In June 1861, she wrote, 'We live on a mine that the Negroes are suspected of an intention to spring on the fourth of next month.'

Like thousands of Southern women, Kate found refuge in prayer groups and religion. In late June after an abundant rain, Kate remarked that the crops were thriving and that 'The North cannot starve us, try as they may, and God will aid us in our righteous cause.' 'May I always be able to put my trust in God ... satisfied that He will order our future as is best ... He has given us wise rulers, brave and successful generals, valiant and patriotic men, and a united people, self-sacrificing and with their trust in God.'

As the war moved closer to northeast Louisiana, Kate's scorn for the Yankees increased. She reported on the sacrifices of Southern planters in late January 1862, commenting that Confederate General Leonidas Polk had called on all the planters along the Mississippi River to send their slaves to assist in fortifying Fort Pillow some 40 miles (64km) north of Memphis. 'Separating the old family Negroes who have lived and worked together for so many years is a great grief to them and a distress to us,' she observed. After reading a January letter from her brother, she came to the realization that 'The manner in which the North is moving her forces, now that she thinks us surrounded and can give us the annihilating blow, reminds me of a party of hunters crouched around the covert of the deer, and when the lines are drawn and there is no escape, they close in and kill.'

Kate reported the fall of Fort Henry and Fort Donelson, and the capture of significant points in Kentucky, Tennessee, and Missouri, which left Vicksburg open from the North. She abhorred the sight of Federal gunboats on the Mississippi River only a few miles from Brokenburn. She lamented the fact that the southern approach to Vicksburg was opened by the fall of New Orleans, Baton Rouge, and Natchez. She was concerned that the loss of the river cities would allow the Union army to 'descend the Mississippi and get all the cotton they can steal.' Benjamin Butler's occupation of New Orleans in April 1862 provoked a fierce reaction. 'It made my blood boil to … think of New Orleans completely in his power.' Kate hoped such losses would inspire the populace. 'All other tidings are gloomy but they have aroused the country with a trumpet call. There is the greatest excitement throughout the country. Almost everyone is going and going at once,' she recorded. 'The whole country is awake and on the watch – think and talk only of war.'

By the summer of 1862, Kate's daily entries focused almost exclusively on military affairs. She was beginning to comprehend the significance of the Union victories of the spring. 'The merchants are selling only for cash and that cash is hard to get, unless we can do as they seem to be doing in the towns – make it,' she observed.

She also wrote of the tension that conscription caused in the Confederacy. 'The conscription has caused a great commotion and great consternation among the shirking stay-at-homes.' 'Around here many are deluding themselves with the belief that the call will not be enforced in Louisiana now that New Orleans has fallen and Vicksburg is threatened.' 'We earnestly hope these coward souls will be made to go … Not a single man has joined for the last two months.'

The surrender of Nashville and the river forts, and much of the Mississippi River, made Kate realize that 'fair Louisiana with her fertile fields of cane and cotton … lies powerless at the feet of the enemy.' 'Though the Yankees have gained the land, the people are determined they shall not have its wealth, and from every plantation rises the smoke of burning cotton.' Her own family burned $20,000 worth in May 1862. Although the planters looked upon the burning of cotton as almost ruin to their fortunes, it must be done for the cause, she argued. As the Union soldiers pressed on to Corinth, Mississippi, Kate invoked the Almighty to produce Confederate success in the west, writing in her diary: 'Grant a victory, Father, we pray.'

Plagued by shortages of food, clothing, and medicines, Kate watched with scorn as the Union army threatened to close Vicksburg in the summer of 1862. 'It seems hopeless to make a stand at Vicksburg,' she wrote. 'We only hope they may burn the city if they meet with any resistance.' 'How much better to burn our cities than let them fall into the enemy's hands.' It seemed that God had answered her prayers as the Confederates blocked Federal attempts to lay siege to Vicksburg in the summer and fall of 1862.

While Kate was entertaining Confederate soldiers at Brokenburn on Christmas Eve 1862, General William T. Sherman with 30,000 men arrived at Milliken's Bend, only a few miles away. In the winter months, his troops swarmed the plantation, confiscating horses and supplies, seizing slaves to work on a new canal and encouraging others to leave their masters. On 26 January 1863, 'preparing to run from the Yankees,' Kate tucked her diary away in the bottom of a packing box, 'with only slight chance of seeing it again.' After going for more than a month without writing an entry, she opened the dairy and wrote of the chaos and violence around her. Such was the violence that she wrote in March, 'For the last two days we have been in a quiver of anxiety for the Yankees every minute.' When the Yankees came on 22 March, she wrote that 'The life we are leading now is a miserable, frightened one – living in constant dread of great danger, not knowing what form it may take, and utterly helpless to protect ourselves.'

While she was visiting a neighbor, an armed slave seized Kate, her little sister, and several other women, forced them into one room, and held them at gunpoint while other slaves looted the house. Though Union authorities forbade planters to leave, this incident convinced Kate's mother that the family must flee.

With only the clothes on their backs, the Stones left Brokenburn on a cold March night. When the family reached Delhi, Louisiana, they found the chaos of a fleeing countryside, 'everybody and everything,' Kate wrote, 'trying to get on the cars, all fleeing from the Yankees or worse still, the Negroes.' Despite the confusion, the Stones finally got on the train and reached Monroe, 80 miles (130km) inland from the Mississippi. There they spent seven weeks before they continued their trek to Texas. To add to Kate's despair, news came of the death of her brother Walter in Mississippi two months earlier. The family would spend the remainder of the war in Texas.

The promise of summer

By the summer of 1863, the war in the Western Theater had produced significant changes. Thousands of soldiers had fought several major battles in the Upper South states, which ultimately kept Missouri and Kentucky in the Union. The North could boast of a series of military successes, including the fall of Forts Henry and Donelson, the victories at Shiloh, Perryville, Iuka, and Stone's River, and the capture and occupation of Nashville, Corinth, Memphis, New Orleans, Port Hudson, and Vicksburg. The cumulative effect of these victories brought tremendous economic hardships to many Confederates and transformed the character of the war.

The Confederate war effort in the west was trapped in a tumultuous cycle that only got worse as the war continued. To be successful against the Union armies in the west, the Confederate government had to resort to coercive measures that centralized its authority over the states. These measures, however, became counterproductive and increased discontent among Southerners, which eroded the morale and strength of the very armies that the controls were designed to benefit. Some soldiers began to feel that the danger in the rear was worse than the danger in the front. Southern soldiers, particularly those in the Army of the Tennessee such as John Magee, were weary of the war. 'This news [Vicksburg] causes a depression of spirits in the whole army,' wrote Magee in July.

The campaigns in the Western Theater in the first two years of the conflict proved invaluable for both armies. With tremendous military experience that few officers on either side could boast of, Albert Sidney Johnston emerged early as the savior of the west, a hero of the republic of Texas, the United States, and the Confederacy. Jefferson Davis referred to him as the 'great pillar of the Confederacy.' In many respects he had been a military idol, and his death at Shiloh left a significant void in the Confederate high command. Braxton Bragg said at the time that 'No one cause probably contributed so greatly to our loss of time, which was the loss of success, as the fall of the commanding general.' Whether the outcome of the battle would have been different had Johnston lived, his death was a turning point in the war in the west. 'Death on the battlefield, after taking Grant by surprise made him a martyred genius in Southern eyes,' argued one scholar; it 'placed a halo around his head,' complained Beauregard.

Thanks to an effective use of combined military operations, the Union held a distinct advantage in the Western Theater, and the experience of war produced an invaluable lesson for conducting the war. Not only had the Union combined army and naval operations successfully, but also it learned that conducting half-hearted campaigns designed to achieve a harmonious peace was losing them the war. At a time when policy makers were beginning to see the advantages of expanding the war, Lincoln and the North found in Grant the military hero they had been seeking to wage a more vigorous war. Though an 'awesomely common man,' as some characterized him, after Vicksburg the commander's star rose rapidly.

Grant also found in William T. Sherman a commander in whom he placed much confidence in carrying out the same kind of war. The two commanders had proven that they could learn from the experience of war, and they supported the total commitment to bringing defeat to the Confederacy. Both were now willing to have their men make war on the South, not just its armies. At a time when the Northern economy and leadership had harnessed the industrial and technological advances, they had military commanders who would utilize these resources and bring the war to a close.

By July 1863, the war seemed almost endless for Southern soldiers. Morale was rapidly plummeting in the Confederacy due to military setbacks. Grant had eliminated an entire army from further military action, yet had sustained fewer than 10,000 casualties himself. Such exploits caused Treasury Secretary Salmon P. Chase to remark to Massachusetts Governor William Sprague, 'Our military prospects now look really bright.' 'The people all along the [Mississippi] River, and throughout the Western Mississippi are abjectly submissive.' Although most Confederates were still committed to Southern independence, they increasingly turned against the Davis administration. The fall of Vicksburg eroded the solidarity of purpose between the civilian populace and Confederate authorities.

The Confederacy could win the war if they went on the offensive and frustrated the Union armies on the field. Victory in the west might turn the Northern populace away from the Lincoln administration and force political leaders to consider a negotiated peace. Though the Union held the upper hand in the west in the summer of 1863, only time would tell if they could sustain their domination in the occupied zones while fighting the Rebels on the field of battle.

Bibliography

Primary sources

Basler, Roy P. (ed.), *Collected Works of Abraham Lincoln*, 8 vols, New Brunswick, 1953–55.

Beatty, John, *The Citizen Soldier; or, Memoirs of a Volunteer*, Cincinnati, Ohio, 1879.

Grant, Ulysses S., *Personal Memoirs of U. S. Grant*, 2 vols, New York, 1885.

Johnson, Robert U., and Clarence C. Buel (eds), *Battles and Leaders of the Civil War*, 4 vols, New York, 1887.

Nevins, Allan, *Diary of George Templeton Strong*, 4 vols, New York, 1952.

Sherman, William T., *Memoirs*, 2 vols, New York, 1875.

Stone, Kate, *Brokenburn: The Journal of Kate Stone, 1861–1868*, Baton Rouge, Louisiana, 1955.

Williams, Frederick D., *The Wild Life of the Army: Civil War Letters of James A. Garfield*, East Lansing, Michigan, 1964.

Secondary sources

Ambrose, Stephen E., *Halleck: Lincoln's Chief of Staff*, Baton Rouge, Louisiana, 1962.

Ash, Stephen V., *Middle Tennessee Society Transformed, 1860–1870*, Baton Rouge, Louisiana, 1988.

Ash, Stephen V., *When the Yankees Came: Conflict and Chaos in the Occupied South, 1861–1865*, Chapel Hill, North Carolina, 1995.

Barney, William L., *Battleground for the Union: The Era of the Civil War and Reconstruction, 1848–1877*, Englewood Cliffs, New Jersey, 1990.

Carter, Samuel, *The Final Fortress: The Campaign for Vicksburg, 1862–1863*, New York, 1980.

Cooling, Benjamin Franklin, *Fort Donelson's Legacy: War and Society in Kentucky and Tennessee, 1862–1863*, Knoxville, Tennessee, 1997.

Cooling, Benjamin Franklin, *Forts Henry and Donelson: The Key to the Confederate Heartland*, Knoxville, Tennessee, 1987.

Cozzens, Peter, *No Better Place to Die: The Battle of Stones River*, Urbana, Illinois, 1990.

Cozzens, Peter, *The Darkest Days of the War: The Battles of Iuka and Corinth*, Chapel Hill, North Carolina, 1997.

Daniel, Larry, *Shiloh: The Battle That Changed the Civil War*, New York, 1997.

Davis, William C., *'A Government of Our Own': The Making of the Confederacy*, New York, 1994.

Donald, David, *Lincoln*, New York, 1995.

Engle, Stephen D., *Don Carlos Buell: Most Promising of All*, Chapel Hill, North Carolina, 1999.

Engle, Stephen D., *Struggle for the Heartland: The Campaigns From Fort Henry to Corinth*, Lincoln, Nebraska, 2001.

Frank, Joseph A., and George K. Reaves, *'Seeing the Elephant': Raw Recruits at the Battle of Shiloh*, New York, 1989.

Grimsley, Mark, *The Hard Hand of War: Union Military Policy Toward Southern Civilians, 1861–1865*, Cambridge, England, Cambridge University Press, 1995.

Hagerman, Edward, *The American Civil War and the Origins of Modern Warfare*, Bloomington, Indiana, 1988.

Hattaway, Herman, and Archer Jones, *How the North Won: A Military History of the Civil War*, Urbana, Illinois, 1983.

Hess, Earl, *Banners to the Breeze: The Kentucky Campaign, Corinth, and Stones River*, Lincoln, Nebraska, 2000.

Klement, Frank L., *The Limits of Dissent: Clement L. Vallandigham and the Civil War*, Lexington, Massachusetts, 1970.

McDonough, James Lee, *Shiloh: In Hell Before Night*, Knoxville, Tennessee, 1977.

McDonough, James Lee, *War in Kentucky: From Shiloh to Perryville*, Knoxville, Tennessee, 1994.

McPherson, James M., *For Cause and Comrades: Why Men Fought in the Civil War*, New York, 1997.

McPherson, James M., *Battle Cry of Freedom: The Civil War Era*, New York, 1988.

McWhiney, Grady, *Braxton Bragg and Confederate Defeat*, New York, 1969.

Marszalek, John F., *Sherman: A Soldier's Passion for Order*, New York, 1993.

Paludan, Philip Shaw, *'A People's Contest': The Union and the Civil War, 1861–1865*, New York, 1988.

Potter, David M., *The Impending Crisis: 1848–1861*, New York, 1976.

Robertson, James I., *Soldiers Blue and Gray*, Columbia, South Carolina, 1988.

Roland, Charles, *An American Iliad: The Story of the Civil War*, New York, 1991.

Roland, Charles, *Albert Sidney Johnston: Soldier of Three Republics*, Austin, Texas, 1964.

Simpson, Brooks D., *Ulysses S. Grant: Triumph Over Adversity, 1822–1865*, Boston, Massachusetts, 2000.

Thomas, Emory M., *The Confederate Nation, 1861–1865*, New York, 1979.

Index

Figures in **bold** refer to illustrations

Other titles in the Essential Histories series

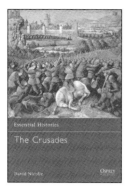

The Crusades
ISBN 1 84176 179 6

available

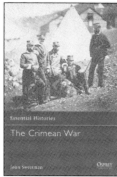

The Crimean War
ISBN 1 84176 186 9

available

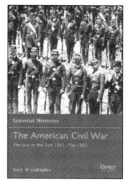

The American Civil War
The war in the East
1861–May 1863
ISBN 1 84176 239 3

available

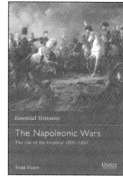

The Napoleonic Wars
The rise of the Emperor
1805–1807
ISBN 1 84176 205 9

available

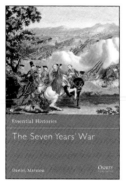

The Seven Years' War
ISBN 1 84176 191 5

available

The American Civil War
The war in the East
1863–1865
ISBN 1 84176 205 9

available

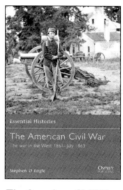

The American Civil War
The war in the West
1861–July 1863
ISBN 1 84176 240 7

available

**The French
Revolutionary Wars**
ISBN 1 84176 283 0

available

The Korean War
ISBN 1 84176 282 2

available

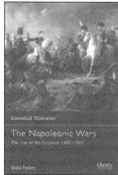

The Napoleonic Wars
The Empires fight back
1808–1812
ISBN 1 84176 298 9

available

The American Civil War
The war in the West
1863–1865
ISBN 1 84176 242 3

November 2001

The Norman Invasion
ISBN 1 84176 228 8

November 2001

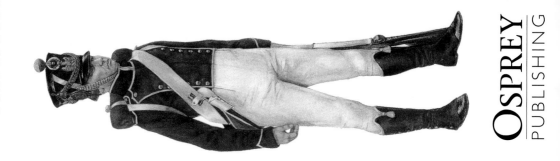

OSPREY
PUBLISHING

FIND OUT MORE ABOUT OSPREY

❏ Please send me a FREE trial issue of Osprey Military Journal

❏ Please send me the latest listing of Osprey's publications

❏ I would like to subscribe to Osprey's e-mail newsletter

Title/rank

Name

Address

Postcode/zip

State/country

E-mail

Which book did this card come from?

❏ I am interested in military history

My preferred period of military history is _____

❏ I am interested in military aviation

My preferred period of military aviation is _____

I am interested in (please tick all that apply)

❏ general history   ❏ militaria   ❏ model making

❏ wargaming   ❏ re-enactment

Please send to:

USA & Canada:
Osprey Direct USA, c/o Motorbooks International,
PO Box 1, 729 Prospect Avenue, Osceola, WI 54020, USA

UK, Europe and rest of world:
Osprey Direct UK, PO Box 140, Wellingborough,
Northants, NN8 2FA, United Kingdom

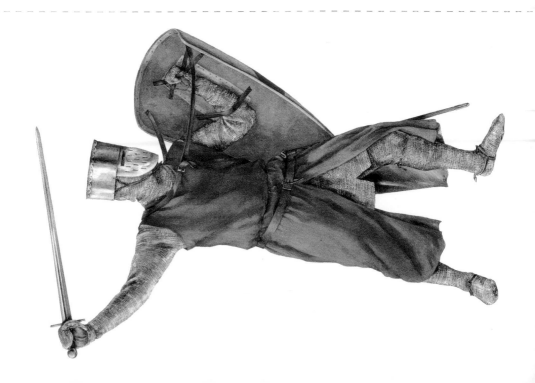

OSPREY
PUBLISHING

www.ospreypublishing.com

call our telephone hotline
for a free information pack

USA & Canada: 1-800-458-0454
UK, Europe and rest of world call:
+44 (0) 1933 443 863

Young Guardsman
Figure taken from *Warrior 22:
Imperial Guardsman 1799–1815*
Published by Osprey
Illustrated by Christa Hook

Knight, c.1190
Figure taken from *Warrior 1: Norman Knight 950 – 1204AD*
Published by Osprey
Illustrated by Christa Hook

POSTCARD